60 Thoughts on
Life's Temptations, Trials,
and Triumphs

OVERCOMING
the HURT

Arnie Cole, Pam Ovwigho & Michael Ross

An Imprint of Barbour Publishing, Inc.

Contents

IS LIFE PEACEFUL? IT'LL CHANGE

In the land of Uz there lived a man whose name was Job.
This man was blameless and upright; he feared God and shunned evil.

JOB 1:1

Faith Quest

Read Job 1:1–3
Where is your focus when life is peaceful?

Faith Trek

In just a few short verses, we learn much about Job. He lived in the land of Uz, part of modern-day Saudi Arabia. And, in short, he had it all: family, material goods, and prestige. He was a father of ten, a landowner, and an employer. His fields were teeming with thousands and thousands of livestock, from sheep and camels to oxen and donkeys. Job, in fact, was the wealthiest man in his region.

Such bounty often comes with a heavy dose of temptation, and Job likely faced his share. Perhaps he was tempted to amass more wealth. Overlooking his vast land and flocks, Job could have congratulated himself on his success. He could have fixed his thoughts and energies on how to grow his riches even more.

Perhaps the siren song of pride rang in his ears. As the richest man in town, he must have received much flattery and many compliments from his friends and neighbors. These words brought the temptation to believe that he alone had created his peaceful and rich life.

Yet Job remained a devout man of faith, with his eyes fixed firmly on his Lord. He lived with integrity, dealing honestly in all his affairs. He deliberately avoided evil. Job feared God, and this awe and reverence for his Creator fueled a life of obedience.

Jesus cautioned that it is very difficult for a rich person to enter the kingdom of heaven (Matthew 19:23). So then, is wealth and the peaceful life it brings inherently evil? Not necessarily. Rather, Jesus is cautioning us about how a comfortable life can lull us spiritually. We may become so focused on enjoying our family, home, and material things that our eyes stray from our Creator. We can, in essence, lose our bearings and compass.

Keeping our focus on God also helps us maintain an eternal perspective and hold the things we have with open hands. Surrounded by his family and his wealth, Job may have been tempted to believe that his life would always be that way. He could have thought that he had "achieved" this good life and thus it was his forever.

As a man of faith, though, he knew that his earthly life was only a small sliver compared to eternity. Similarly, I (Pam) sometimes catch myself clinging to the good times in my life, hoping that the seas will remain smooth. Yet in my heart I know better. Inevitably, a medical test comes back positive, a job ends, or some other storm enters our lives. I've learned that keeping the Lord as the center of my life in peaceful times is critical to weathering these storms.

Through consistent nurturing of our relationship with our Lord, we come to know who He is. We develop a deep understanding of His character, that He is eternal, faithful, and loving. Daily encounters remind us that He is with us always (Matthew 28:20). Walking closely with God during the peaceful times of life provides an anchor for our soul, an anchor that is sorely needed because a storm could be just over the horizon.

Faith Tools

- The peaceful times in life are a blessing to enjoy with the understanding that things will not always be so.
- Staying focused on our relationship with the Lord during the peaceful times of life prepares us to face the coming storms.

- **Pray**: "Lord, help me focus on You during the peaceful times." Thank God for the many blessings in your life. Ask Him for the strength and perseverance to avoid the temptations that come with a peaceful life. Seek His strength to walk in obedience and remain focused on Him in all seasons.

Notes for Growth

A Key Point I Learned Today:

_____

_____

_____

How I Want to Grow:

_____

_____

_____

My Prayer List:

_____

_____

_____

SPIRITUAL LEADERSHIP IN THE GOOD TIMES

And when the days of the feast had run their course, Job would send and consecrate them, and he would rise early in the morning and offer burnt offerings according to the number of them all. For Job said, "It may be that my children have sinned, and cursed God in their hearts." Thus Job did continually.

JOB 1:5 ESV

Faith Quest

Read Job 1:4–5
How do I lead spiritually in the "good times"?

Faith Trek

Job's wealth provided an easy life for him—and an easy life for his ten children. While others were striving for their livelihood, whether out in the field with the sheep or in a trade, Job's adult sons and daughters had time to spare. Some of that time was spent holding extravagant parties. Not only did these parties span many days, but they also rotated among the sons' houses.

These two verses give a glimpse of Job as a father and a spiritual leader. We can glean that he was generous with his children, sharing the wealth that he had accumulated. His sons presumably had married and established their own homes. Whether directly or indirectly, his riches likely provided for the food and drink at their bashes.

Job understood that his children needed times of fun and relaxation. But, as a spiritual leader, he also understood that they needed God. He reflected on how his children's easy lives could have tempted them to sin. He knew they needed cleansing from their sins.

Thus, Job was proactive in nurturing the spiritual lives of his children. Scripture does not tell us the details of their daily lives. I (Pam) imagine that Job led his children by example in his own prayer life and devotion to his Lord. I can just picture him sitting around the campfire surrounded by his sons and daughters, sharing with them about God.

His spiritual leadership didn't stop once they were grown and off on their own. Verse 5 points out that his regular practice was to call them to a time of worship and cleansing when their celebrations were completed.

How does Job's example fit with how we as parents disciple our children today? One difference is that our society focuses quite a bit on happiness—our own and our children's. As some psychologists note, many homes have become child-centric, with the primary focus on the children's needs, wants, and activities. Giving our children things they enjoy, seeing their smiles, and hearing their laughter warms our hearts. Yet we can't let providing these pleasures and comforts distract us from our primary purpose.

In these verses from Job, we're reminded that, just as an easy life can make us spiritually lazy, it can also have the same effect on our children. They need us to care for them, lead them, and teach them about the risks that come with an easy life. Just as Job did, we must keep pointing them to God, the One who loves them, saves them, and will sustain them in the not-so-easy times.

Faith Tools

- Spiritual leadership includes helping our children nurture their relationships with God when life is easy.
- Just as Job, we can lead by example and by actively calling our children to worship.
- **Pray:** "Lord, strengthen me to lead others during the peaceful times." Thank God for the people He has put in your life to lead and disciple. Ask Him for the sensitivity to know where each person is spiritually and the wisdom to guide them. Encourage those you are leading to walk in obedience and remain focused on Him in all seasons.

Notes for Growth

A Key Point I Learned Today:

_____

_____

_____

How I Want to Grow:

_____

_____

_____

My Prayer List:

_____

_____

_____

WHEN GOOD PEOPLE AND BAD THINGS COLLIDE

And the LORD said to Satan, "Have you considered my servant Job,
that there is none like him on the earth, a blameless and upright man,
who fears God and turns away from evil?"

JOB 1:8 ESV

Faith Quest

Read Job 1:6–12
How often do you consider what's going on in the spiritual realms?

Faith Trek

In this set of verses, the focus shifts from Job's earthly life to the invisible spiritual realm. Imagine it as a stage performance and you may picture a change from bright meadows with birds singing to an ethereal, smoky world with powerful, slightly ominous musical overtones. If you've read Job before, you may feel uneasiness in the pit of your stomach as you anticipate that Job's life is about to change in a very big, very bad way.

God has called together his angelic beings. Satan is among them and, when asked, reports that he has been roaming up and down the earth. Like a lion on the prowl, he is on the hunt. And Job ends up being the one in his sights.

The strength of Job's relationship with God is evident in these verses. Similar to how an excited father would respond when talking to a friend who recently visited his son's college, God asks Satan, "Have you seen Job?" He goes on to say that Job is like no one else in that he is blameless, upright, fearing God and turning away from evil.

Satan's response is chilling. He lives up to his nickname "the accuser" as he launches a direct assault on Job's character. He has indeed noticed Job and is not impressed at all by his devout life. If this were a court case, Satan's argument would go something like this:

> Members of the jury, do not let Job's respectable clothes and impressive résumé fool you. Sin and selfishness pervade his heart just as they do any other man's heart. Sure, he appears to love and worship God. But look at his life! God has bought Job's devotion by giving him this rich and easy life. Take those things away and he will turn from God, just like everyone else.

Now put your name in place of Job's. Satan is an equal opportunity accuser, ready to attack anyone and everyone who chooses to follow Christ. Satan is not all knowing as our God is. Yet he is an astute observer of human behavior. Here he is pointing out that good people often stumble when bad things happen.

Several years ago we (Arnie and Pam) surveyed kids and teens about how they believed they communicated with God and how He communicated with them. One of the most common answers among these young people was that God communicated with them through the good things in their lives. That is, because they had a home, parents who cared for them, and met needs, they knew God cared for them.

Their responses led to an important question: what would happen to these kids' faith when a storm came? If they lost their home in a fire or one of their parents died in a car accident, would they still hear God's voice, or would they turn away?

Going back to Job, we can ask the same question. Would Job turn from God if the hedge of protection was removed? Our Father, who knew Job better than Job knew himself, answered Satan with confidence: "Behold, all that he has is in your hand. Only against him do not stretch out your hand" (Job 1:12 ESV).

Faith Tools

- Through good times and bad, God wants to have a relationship with each of us.
- Good people may stumble in their faith when bad things detonate their lives.
- **Pray**: "Lord, help me to understand the immense depth of Your love for me, in good times and bad." Thank God for the immense love He has for you and His Word that helps you hear His voice always. Ask Him to strengthen your faith and to give you the ability to keep your eyes on Him when bad things happen. Seek out the Bible verses that comfort you most. Keep them handy for when storms come.

Notes for Growth

A Key Point I Learned Today:

_____

_____

_____

How I Want to Grow:

_____

_____

_____

My Prayer List:

_____

_____

_____

LOSS OF OUR LIVELIHOOD

"Trust in the Lord forever, for the Lord God is an everlasting rock."
Isaiah 26:4 esv

Faith Quest

Read Job 1:13–16
How do you respond when your livelihood is threatened?

Faith Trek

Unaware of what was happening in the spiritual realm, Job went about his activities as usual. Imagine him sitting with his wife around the fire, watching the sunrise and discussing the day ahead. All the kids were heading to their oldest brother's house for a feast. Perhaps the parents chuckled to themselves about how the siblings that fought so much when they were little had now grown to be the best of friends. A group of workers herded the cattle and donkeys to one side of the land, while shepherds guided the sheep to another pasture. Just a typical day on Job's ranch.

Arrival of the first message shattered the serene ordinariness as Job learned that his cattle and donkeys and the servants caring for them were all gone. The first impact of bad news shakes us up. It sets our mind racing. Reeling from the news, Job thought, *How can this be? I just saw them this morning. Why would the Sabeans attack? Surely some have survived. At least we still have the sheep.*

And then the second messenger arrived. A fire from heaven had consumed the sheep and the shepherds, save one. Now he knew the cold hard facts: his livelihood was completely gone.

It's easy to imagine the heartache Job felt. For most of us, our finances and livelihood are close to our hearts. Our careers become part of our identities, often the first thing a new acquaintance asks about. Livelihood represents temporal security for us and our families; it's how we provide for food, shelter, clothing, smartphones, and all of the other necessities of life. Losing employment and business failures can devastate us.

Although our losses may not be as complete as Job's, most of us will experience losses related to our livelihood at some point. Whether the loss comes through a pink slip from our boss or a fire that destroys our business, facing them requires a strong measure of faith and trust in our Lord.

When we (Pam's family) had to close down our family business, discouragement and worry were huge temptations for me. My mind would fill with the "What ifs" each night—what if the business property doesn't sell? What if we can't pay the mortgage this month? I learned to fight these "What ifs" with reminders that we worship Jehovah Jireh, the Lord who provides. He knew that we had a mortgage to pay and four children to feed and clothe. And provide He did, often in amazing ways.

We also had to remind ourselves that we are not our possessions or our jobs. It was indeed a little awkward when we would meet someone new and not have an easy, quick answer to the "What do you do?" question. We couldn't say, "We worry and we wait," though that felt at times like what we were doing. Keeping our focus on Jesus was a powerful reminder that our livelihood is a temporary thing of this world and not who we really are. Rather, our identity rests in Christ, and we must look to Him as we navigate our uncertain future.

Faith Tools

- Our God is Jehovah Jireh, the Lord who provides. He doesn't change even when our circumstances do.
- While society may view our jobs as who we are, our true identity is in Jesus Christ.
- **Pray**: "Lord, thank You for providing for me. Help me to

continue looking to You as my provider." Thank God for all of the ways in which He provides for you. Ask Him to help you to hold your finances and material possessions with open hands. Seek to keep an eternal perspective on your livelihood and to always remember that God is Jehovah Jireh.

Notes for Growth

A Key Point I Learned Today:

_____

_____

_____

How I Want to Grow:

_____

_____

_____

My Prayer List:

_____

_____

_____

LOSS OF A LOVED ONE

The Lord is near to the brokenhearted and saves the crushed in spirit.

PSALM 34:18 ESV

Faith Quest

Read Job 1:17–19

How does the loss of a loved one test your faith?

Faith Trek

The loss of a loved one causes pain beyond words, leaving a giant hole in our hearts and our lives. In these verses, Job experienced that hurt ten times over as he learned that all of his children had perished.

Our bodies are perishable; that fact is unavoidable. Yet whether its approach is seen from a distance in the form of a terminal illness or it comes suddenly as a great wind across the wilderness (Job 1:19), death deals a cruel blow. When a loved one dies, we have many practical details to deal with—people to notify, funeral arrangements to make, and the deceased's belongings to distribute. These details provide some distractions in the early days of grief, giving us something to focus on and do. They don't take away from the fact, though, that we now must go on living without this person who meant so much to us.

Losing a loved one can test our faith. We may question why a loving God would allow this tragedy. It may bring to mind our own mortality and what will happen to us when we die. Some come out of this grieving period with a stronger faith. Others remained trapped in anger and resentment. How do we hold on to our faith through loss?

During His time on earth, Jesus experienced the loss of loved ones. Many theologians believe that His earthly father, Joseph, died before Jesus began His ministry. The Gospels report three instances of Jesus raising someone from the dead. When He encountered a widow in Nain who was burying her son, Jesus had compassion for her (Luke 7:11–17). He reassured Jairus that his daughter would be well (Luke 8:50). Seeing the grief of Mary and Martha at the death of Lazarus, Jesus wept (John 11:35).

These verses can provide comfort when we are grieving our own losses. They reassure us that we have a Savior who understands our pain. Our Lord is not surprised by our tears and sends His Spirit to comfort us as we mourn.

The death of a Christ follower also has a particular bittersweet quality. It brings the pain and loss of departure combined with the hope of a future reunion. Paul wrote in 1 Thessalonians 4:13–14 (NLT):

> *And now, dear brothers and sisters, we want you to know what will happen to the believers who have died so you will not grieve like people who have no hope. For since we believe that Jesus died and was raised to life again, we also believe that when Jesus returns, God will bring back with him the believers who have died.*

For many churches, this hope is reflected in the practice of referring to funerals as a "home going" service. Remembering that death is not the end of the story for a believer and that our loved one who knew Jesus in life is now rejoicing in His presence provides a measure of comfort.

Faith Tools

- Loss of a loved one can test our faith in a loving God.
- Jesus comforts us in our grief and reminds us of the hope we have in life everlasting with Him.
- **Pray**: "Lord, it's so hard to lose the people I cherish. Please comfort me in my grief and help me to trust You amid the tears." Thank God for the special people in your life and for all of the joyful memories you have created together. Ask Him to guide you in how to help those around you who

arc grieving. Always remember the hope of everlasting life through Jesus.

Notes for Growth

A Key Point I Learned Today:

_____

_____

_____

How I Want to Grow:

_____

_____

_____

My Prayer List:

_____

_____

_____

SETBACKS ARE NEVER EASY

And he said, "Naked I came from my mother's womb,
and naked shall I return. The LORD gave, and the LORD
has taken away; blessed be the name of the LORD."

JOB 1:21 ESV

Faith Quest

Read Job 1:20–22
Can you worship in the storm?

Faith Trek

Starting with Job 1:20, we begin to see Job's reaction to the tragic messages he had received. Does anything surprise you in these verses? If you've studied Old Testament customs, you probably already know that tearing one's clothes was a common sign of grief. Shaving of the beard was a mark of sadness for men as well.

And then he fell to the ground and worshipped the Lord.

That last part takes my breath away. Faced with the biggest setback of his life, Job turned to his Lord in worship. When I (Pam) think back to the setbacks I've experienced, I'm sad to admit that focusing on God, His glory and holiness, was usually not my initial reaction. Storms and tragedies tend to spur me into action. Rather than pausing to worship, I'm comforting others, making phone calls, and arranging details. Perhaps these actions are to avoid the pain. Perhaps they are attempts to control what is ultimately an uncontrollable situation.

What about you? Maybe setbacks immobilize you, with all your energies directed inward as you try to emotionally process the pain and shock of what has happened.

Job felt that pain too; this is why he tore his clothes and shaved his beard. Yet he didn't turn those emotions inward. He didn't focus his energy outward and jump into action. Rather, he turned his focus up—to his Lord. Job's relationship with God was so close that turning to the Lord in the midst of overwhelming grief was natural.

The terrorist attacks of September 11, 2001 sent waves of shock and grief all across the country. As people heard the news, a common reaction was to connect with family immediately. Many were also drawn to the church for prayer and comfort in the midst of an unfathomable tragedy.

Similarly, in this passage, Job was seeking comfort from his Lord. He had just heard the worst news of his life, and he was running into the arms of his best friend.

Worshipping the Lord at this moment also gave Job some reassurance. Although everything in his world had just changed, one thing remained the same. God was still God, Alpha, Omega, everlasting.

In verse 21, Job stated eternal truth: everything we have on this earth is from the Lord. And inevitably some things will be taken away, and we will experience the pain of loss. Still we bless God's name for who He is. And knowing that His love for us never gives up and never runs out, we can boldly run to Him amid our setbacks.

Faith Tools

- In the pain of a setback, we have a choice to turn our focus inward, outward, or upward on our Lord.
- Worshipping in the midst of a storm becomes a more natural reaction when it's already a regular part of our lives.
- **Pray**: "Abba Father, you are holy, Lord God Almighty. You alone are worthy of worship." Thank God for being a mighty refuge at all times. Seek to set aside time throughout your week to worship Him. Identify and memorize one or two key Bible verses that will remind you to turn upward when setbacks come.

Notes for Growth

Key Point I Learned Today:

_____

_____

_____

How I Want to Grow:

_____

_____

_____

My Prayer List:

_____

_____

_____

SUFFERING IS INESCAPABLE

*And the LORD said to Satan, "Have you considered my servant Job,
that there is none like him on the earth, a blameless and upright man,
who fears God and turns away from evil? He still holds fast his integrity,
although you incited me against him to destroy him without reason."*

JOB 2:3 ESV

Faith Quest

Read Job 2:1–3
Do you believe that sometimes suffering happens "without reason"?

Faith Trek

Much to Satan's disappointment, Job passed the test. He held strong
to his faith, his integrity, and his God through the painful loss of his
livelihood and loved ones. If this were a movie, we'd all be cheering at
this point for the triumph of the hero!

Back in the heavenly realms, Satan appeared again before God. The
Lord knew what Job had gone through and how he had fared. In fact,
in verse 3, He points out that Job is still blameless, upright, and holding
fast to his integrity.

He also points out that Satan had incited Him against Job to "destroy him without reason." Indeed Satan is the one who wanted to take
away Job's livelihood and loved ones, to try to force him to turn away
from God. Yet the Lord allowed this happen. He also put limits on
Satan, telling him to not touch Job's physical body.

The "without reason" part of verse 3 alludes to a somber truth: suffering and losses occur often for "no reason" and thus are inescapable.

Understanding this truth can have a profound impact on our daily
lives. Many of us today are struggling with a long list of worries about

our families, our finances, our health, and myriad other matters. This worry wears down our bodies, unsettles our minds, and distracts our spirits from focusing on Jesus.

Why do we worry? One major factor is that so many things in life are out of our control—and we're not too comfortable with that. We like to know what will happen tomorrow, that if we do X it will always lead to Y, and, more importantly, if we follow certain rules or avoid certain things, the tragedies of life will just pass over us.

Similarly, when a loss occurs, whether our own or a friend's, we spend time asking "Why?" On one hand, we're trying to understand and absorb what happened. At a deeper level though, we want to know so that we can avoid that type of suffering in the future.

As I (Pam) write this, a news story is airing about a nine-year-old girl who accidentally killed her shooting instructor with a fully automatic Uzi. I catch myself wondering why she was at the shooting range, why she was using such a powerful weapon that is normally restricted to adults, whether there should be more laws in place, and so on.

Here's the problem: I'm wasting energy looking for the reason for a tragic event that is ultimately without reason. This energy is better spent praying for both affected families. I'm pretending that suffering is escapable when it ultimately is not.

So how does understanding this truth on a deep spiritual level help us in overcoming the hurts in life? It can keep us from blaming ourselves or others for the pain. We can avoid the guilt and lashing out at others that make a painful situation even worse. We are freed to move on to healing when we aren't weighed down by looking for someone to blame.

Faith Tools

- The natural human tendency is to look for an explanation for suffering.
- Accepting the hard truth that suffering is inescapable frees us for healing.

- **Pray** : "Lord, suffering is the hardest reality of life. At times it seems even harder because we don't have an explanation for the pain. Help me to understand and accept these truths, trusting that You ultimately are in control."

Notes for Growth

Key Point I Learned Today:

_____

_____

_____

How I Want to Grow:

_____

_____

_____

My Prayer List:

_____

_____

_____

SELF-PITY OR SURRENDER?

But he said to me, "My grace is sufficient for you, for my power is made perfect in weakness." Therefore I will boast all the more gladly of my weaknesses, so that the power of Christ may rest upon me.

2 CORINTHIANS 12:9 ESV

Faith Quest

Read Job 2:4–6
Can you worship in the storm?

Faith Trek

If you've ever wondered what Satan is really after, just read Job. Satan made it crystal clear that his goal was to turn Job away from God. Now he wanted to use another tool from his bag of tricks: physical pain.

Our Lord has created us in a wonderfully marvelous way with body, mind, and spirit all interconnected. What affects one of these areas of our being often spills over into the others. Physical discomfort and pain, these warning signals from our bodies that something is wrong, in particular can cause feelings of anxiety and depression. It can also affect our spiritual lives, distracting us from prayer and leading us to question God's love for us.

This is especially true when the pain is extreme or chronic. It can limit our physical activities, our ability to sleep or concentrate, constricting and consuming our lives. It is estimated that 100 million people suffer with chronic pain in the United States alone. This number is more than the sufferers of diabetes, heart disease, and cancer combined. For these individuals, finding ways to cope physically, emotionally, and spiritually are critical.

The apostle Paul wrote about his own experiences with pain in

2 Corinthians 12:7–10. Although Paul didn't give specifics, he described a thorn in his flesh, "a messenger of Satan to harass me" (v. 7 ESV). Rather than letting the pain drive him away from God, Paul turned to him in prayer. He openly shared what was on his heart and gave up on trying to deal with it in his own human strength. The answer Paul received was not the removal of the thorn, yet it provided a deeper level of spiritual comfort: "My grace is sufficient for you, for my power is made perfect in weakness" (v. 9 ESV). With these words, our Lord reminds us that whatever pain we are going through, His grace covers it all. These words of hope encourage us not to let our physical pains pull us down into self-pity. Instead, He encourages us to rely on His strength and grace to continue to nurture our spirits.

Faith Tools

- Physical pain can constrict our lives by limiting our activities, hijacking our emotions, and dampening our spirits.
- Our Lord's promise that His grace is sufficient helps us overcome the damage of physical pain.
- **Pray**: "My Lord, thank You for the wonderful way You have made me. I ask for Your help today to deal with the pains I experience. Father, let me turn to You in times of weakness and fully draw from Your strength." Make a list of things that you can do, think about, listen to, read, remember, and so on when you're in physical pain and in danger of having it become all consuming.

Notes for Growth

Key Point I Learned Today:

_____

_____

_____

How I Want to Grow:

_____

_____

_____

My Prayer List:

_____

_____

_____

WHEN THE HURT IS UNJUST

*But he said to her, "You speak as one of the foolish women would speak.
Shall we receive good from God, and shall we not receive evil?"
In all this Job did not sin with his lips.*

JOB 2:10 ESV

Faith Quest

Read Job 2:7–10
When is it hardest to hold fast to your integrity?

Faith Trek

Sadly, Job now had to deal with physical pain and weeping sores on top of grieving the loss of his children and livelihood. We've seen that Job's initial response was to worship God rather than turning from God as Satan predicted. Now we get a glimpse into how his wife reacted.

We are told that she asked Job why he was still holding on to his integrity. Then she advised him to curse God and die. These were pretty harsh words, especially from his spouse.

My (Pam's) heart softens a bit toward Job's wife, though, when I reflect on the fact that she had experienced the same painful losses, too. Her livelihood was inseparable from her husband's and thus gone with the Sabeans and the fire. Moreover, those were her children who perished when the house crashed down around them. Now she witnessed the love of her life suffering with a horrid sickness.

We aren't told anything about Mrs. Job's relationship with God. Perhaps her faith had been as strong as her husband's and she had joined him in worship. Maybe it was shakier.

Sadly, her words suggest that, at the very least, the tragedies scattered whatever faith she did have. Through her pain, she couldn't see any reason to follow God. Job's continued devotion was incomprehensible to her in the midst of their suffering. Thus she couldn't help but tell him that he should just give it up.

Job's answer provides an important faith lesson for all of us. He returned again to the fact that he worshipped God for *who* He is, not because of what He does or gives. He acknowledged that basing his faith on the Lord's holiness and righteousness rendered the ups and downs of life somewhat irrelevant. Yes, he still experienced those ups and downs. He felt the joys, the sorrows, and the pain. While he may have cried out to God in his pain or wondered why these things were happening, Job realized that God was still God and worthy of worship.

Faith Tools

- Holding fast to our faith can be difficult in times of trouble and when others around us are falling away.
- Remembering that we worship God for who He is helps when hurts tempt us to turn away.
- **Pray**: "Lord, please forgive me for those times when I get too caught up in what You give to me instead of who You are. Thank You for loving me so much that You sent Your Son to die for me. Help me to navigate the storms of life with integrity." Spend a little time today reflecting on how you have responded to the unjust hurts in your life. Talk to God about those times and how you can move past any hurt that remains.

Notes for Growth

Key Point I Learned Today:

_____

_____

_____

How I Want to Grow:

_____

_____

_____

My Prayer List:

_____

_____

_____

_____

YOU ARE NOT ALONE

*They made an appointment together to come
to show him sympathy and comfort him.*

JOB 2:11 ESV

Faith Quest

Read Job 2:11
Is your life open enough to comfort a friend in need?

Faith Trek

Even in ancient times, news traveled. We learn in verse 11 that Job's three friends Eliphaz, Bildad, and Zophar had heard of the tragedies that occurred in his life. Their response went beyond simply sending a message of sympathy or adding Job to their temple's prayer list. They took action. Specifically, they went to Job to comfort him.

Given how their names are listed, it's likely the three friends lived in different areas. They had to make arrangements to travel and for someone to attend to their affairs while they were gone. They met at some central point and then traveled together to see Job.

Stop for a moment and think about how you would respond in their circumstances. We are blessed to live in a time when communication and travel are much easier. Yet are our lives open enough so that we can drop everything to respond to a friend in need?

The comfort of a friend soothes the soul like nothing else. Friends share in our pain and comfort us with their hugs, words, prayers, and silent presence. A friend can give us hope when we are hopeless.

Perhaps more than anything else, they remind us that we are not alone. As Solomon notes in Ecclesiastes 4:10 (ESV), two are better than one because, "if they fall, one will lift up his fellow, but woe to him who is alone when he falls and has not another to lift him up!" In modern times, people struggling with various issues from domestic violence to depression to grief, find comfort and encouragement in formal support groups. The power of these groups largely stems from their ability to reinforce the truth that the sufferer is not alone.

If you are struggling with hurt today, please be encouraged that you are not alone. Seek out others who can come alongside you and give you the support you need. That may be through friends, family, or even a formal support group.

Also be encouraged by Job's friends to reach out to those around you. Do you see someone hurting today? You may be the one God is calling to comfort that person.

Faith Tools

- Job's friends sacrificed their own comfort and convenience to help a friend in need.
- We can look to others to remind us in times of trouble that we are not alone.
- **Pray**: "Lord, times of trouble can trick me into thinking that I'm alone. I ask You to help me graciously accept the help of friends and to always remember that I'm not alone." Thank God for the people in your life who provide comfort when you are in pain. Ask Him to give you a spirit that is sensitive and responsive to those around you who are also hurting.

Notes for Growth

Key Point I Learned Today:

_____

_____

_____

How I Want to Grow:

_____

_____

_____

My Prayer List:

_____

_____

_____

EMPATHY, NOT CONDEMNATION

And they sat with him on the ground seven days and seven nights, and no one spoke a word to him, for they saw that his suffering was very great.

JOB 2:13 ESV

Faith Quest

Read Job 2:12–13
Never underestimate the power of presence.

Faith Trek

When Job's friends saw him from a distance, they were overwhelmed. They were likely used to seeing their wealthy friend nicely groomed, healthy and fit, and in good spirits. Now they saw him with his clothes torn and beard shorn, sitting in the dust weeping. They responded with empathy rather than sympathy. They, too, tore their clothes and began to weep. They joined Job, sitting in the dirt.

Perhaps even more remarkable is that they spent the next seven days and nights sitting with him without saying a word. Whether this was intentional or just a sign of their overwhelming grief, we'll never know. It's telling, though, in that it illustrates the power of just being present with a hurting friend.

One of our ministry staff at Back to the Bible, Sam, shared a poignant memory about such an experience from his own life. He shares how his father's coworker, Art, responded when Sam's mother was dying. He writes:

> *When things got bad, everyone flew in. Aunts, cousins, grandparents. They were full of distractions—trips to the zoo, cigarettes, loud jokes.*

*Dad spent most nights in the hospital room alone,
doing his best to look death in the eyes. When Art fin-
ished his shift at 3:00 a.m., he would join Dad, hat in
hand, working the cigar in the corner of his mouth. They
didn't talk, but Art came almost every night and sat,
reading his King James Bible in the eerie loneliness of
that awful room.*

*And I don't mean to slight anyone else who was
there—who can blame them?—but all the casseroles and
condolences didn't mean much. Art was simply present,
offering no critiques or advice. He would occasionally
weep, occasionally pray, and then he would leave Dad
sleeping fitfully in the thinly padded hospital chair.*

*I learned a lot that Christmas. It was a dark time,
chaotic and unraveling. I learned what fear and death
looked like. But through Art, and others like him, I
learned what love looked like, too. I learned why Jesus
cried at a funeral. I learned that sometimes the only
thing that should be offered is silence.*

Perhaps it was the comforting presence of friends that led Jesus to take
Peter, James, and John with him when he went to pray in the garden
of Gethsemane. As he faced the sacrifice to come, he didn't seek their
words of comfort, but rather just their companionship.

Similarly, Job's friends provide a poignant example of how to respond to a friend in need. Through sharing in Job's grief and being pow-
erfully present, they provide a humbling example of what friendship is.

Faith Tools

- Job's friends displayed empathy in response to his suffering.
- Often we provide the most comfort to those who are hurting
  by our silent presence.
- **Pray**: "Lord, I know that You have promised never to leave

me or forsake me. I cherish that promise. Help me to follow Your spirit in comforting others, whether that is through words or simply my silent presence."

Notes for Growth

Key Point I Learned Today:

_____

_____

_____

How I Want to Grow:

_____

_____

_____

My Prayer List:

_____

_____

_____

JOB'S LAMENT NO. 1: WHY HAS EVERYTHING SOURED?

After this, Job opened his mouth and cursed the day of his birth.
He said: "May the day of my birth perish, and the night it was said,
'A boy is conceived!' That day—may it turn to darkness;
may God above not care about it; may no light shine on it."

JOB 3:1–4

Faith Quest

Read Job 3:1–10
When bad things happen, do you shake your fist at God—or lean into
Him?

Faith Trek

"Obliterate the day I was born. Blank out the night I was conceived!
Let it be a black hole in space. May God above forget it ever happened.
Erase it from the books! May the day of my birth be buried in deep
darkness, shrouded by the fog, swallowed by the night" (Job 3:1–4 MSG).

Eugene H. Peterson perfectly captures Job's anguish in *The Message*,
echoing what we might say if we had to endure his pain. "What's the
point of life?" we may ask—just as Job did. "If this is how my life is going to be, then I wish I had never been born."

Others might shake an angry fist at God: "Why, Lord? Why would
You do this to me?"

The happiness Job once savored because of God's favor was now
gone, and his very existence had quickly turned into an intolerable bur-
den. We see in verse 3 that he veered close to cursing God yet didn't do
it. Job stopped short.

A few years back, I (Michael) helplessly watched as cancer grad-
ually stole my brother's life. Jerry battled the disease for nearly two
years—twenty-four hellish months of blood tests, MRIs, CT scans,

PET scans, simple X-rays, physical therapies. Poking. Probing. Jabbing. Injecting. He was constantly visiting chemical oncologists, radiologists, and pulmonologists; he underwent countless surgical procedures; and he spent thousands and thousands of dollars on drugs—some that appeared to do more harm than good, others that promised to be the "silver bullet" against cancer. Yet, despite an all-out medical assault, my once robust brother was steadily withering away—turning into a listless, emaciated patient—a victim of a terminal illness.

I had to accept what I'd tried hard to deny: Jerry was dying.

"I'm so sorry," I said to him as we talked by phone one evening. "I'm so very sorry. I think you can beat this. You've fought so hard."

"I'm tired, Mike. . .very tired." He paused and then spoke again, a bit more reflective. "I've tried to do some good in this life, to help people, to be there for them—"

"Yes, you have. You've been there for me."

"I don't think I'm going to make it."

"I'll keep praying."

"Pray. Yes—please do. And know that I love you. That's why I called. I just wanted to tell you that."

"I love you, too."

"I've got to hang up now. . .got to go."

"Good-bye, Jerry."

"Good-bye."

As my brother's name faded from the screen on my cell phone, I sat in disbelief. *Is that it? Are those the last words I'll ever say to him?*

Fortunately, I got to share a few more moments with him, even a priceless Thanksgiving visit I'll always hold in my heart. But I can't sugarcoat the last days of his life. They were painful—for Jerry and for those of us who watched him slip away. On one particular afternoon, my brother couldn't hold back his emotions. Unlike Job who stopped short of cursing God, Jerry crossed that line.

My heart melted.

Yet I sensed the Lord telling me, *I've got this. I'm God, and Jerry is in My arms. I understand his pain. . .and I love him deeply.*

Right there in that desperate moment, the truth of Romans

8:38–39 rang crystal clear:

For I am convinced that neither death nor life, neither angels nor demons, neither the present nor the future, nor any powers, neither height nor depth, nor anything else in all creation, will be able to separate us from the love of God that is in Christ Jesus our Lord.

Faith Tools

- Remember that Jesus has big arms. He understands your pain, your grief. He cares, and He's right there with you.
- Like Job, cry out to the Lord. Don't be afraid to share your pain.
- **Pray**: "O Lord my God, I praise Your holy name. I know You are with me and my loved ones. Draw us closer to You." Ask the Lord to help you lean into Him as the pain intensifies.

Notes for Growth

Key Point I Learned Today:

_____

_____

_____

How I Want to Grow:

_____

_____

_____

My Prayer List:

_____

_____

_____

JOB'S LAMENT NO. 2: WHY WAS I BORN INTO THIS?

He heals the brokenhearted
and binds up their wounds.
PSALM 147:3

Faith Quest

Read Job 3:11–15
How does God bring healing to those who are crushed in spirit?

Faith Trek

At one time or another, we've all mouthed Job's desperate pleas.

And, admittedly, we know that our emotions don't always match our grievances—like when we lash out because we don't get our way, or during those moments when we feel inconvenienced. *Oh great, the car won't start. And now I'm late dropping off the kids at school. . .and late for work. . .and will probably end up dumping money that I don't have into this stupid piece of junk. My life stinks! Why, Lord—why was I born into this?*

But on some occasions our anguish is justified—as in Job's case. He had to endure the unthinkable: loss, destruction, physical pain.

I (Michael) met a modern-day Job.

Several years back, I was on assignment for Focus on the Family, writing an article about a burn victim named Brian. He was barely out of his teen years with his whole life ahead of him, yet a fire at his work altered his life.

To keep Brian alive, surgeons had to sacrifice his infected limbs. He endured nineteen surgeries—nearly one per week during his stay at a burn center—as well as multiple skin grafts. The accident left him blind and his body disfigured.

On the day that I interviewed this young man, his mom wheeled him into his family's living room, right next to my chair, and his girlfriend (now his wife) held a straw to his mouth so he could take sips of Coke as we talked. I asked numerous questions; they seemed to roll off my tongue. I was mesmerized by his story. He answered each one—very honestly.

Brian was relaxed, at peace. He smiled a lot and laughed a few times. He shared about how much he loved God and his family. . .and how excited he was about the future.

No bitterness.

No fear.

No worry.

I instantly thought about my own life and the many inconveniences that I complain about. Suddenly, my problems seemed so petty compared with Brian's challenges.

The Psalms have a thing or two to say about God's love for us during hard times:

> *Psalm 10:17:* "*You, Lord, hear the desire of the afflicted; you encourage them, and you listen to their cry.*"
> *Psalm 23:4 (ESV):* "*Even though I walk through the valley of the shadow of death, I will fear no evil, for you are with me; your rod and your staff, they comfort me.*"
> *Psalm 126:5:* "*Those who sow with tears will reap with songs of joy.*"

Faith Tools

- Jesus knows everything about you, and yet He's crazy in love with you. He died for you so you can spend eternity with Him (see 1 John 4:7–16).
- Jesus tells you to let go. He can be trusted; He will take care of us and help us overcome the struggles we face (see 1 John 5:1–5).

- **Pray**: "Lord, restore my hope when life feels so hopeless. Help me to handle life's problems—both big and small." Ask God to change your attitude.

Notes for Growth

Key Point I Learned Today:

_____

_____

_____

How I Want to Grow:

_____

_____

_____

My Prayer List:

_____

_____

_____

JOB'S LAMENT NO. 3:
WHY CAN'T I DIE INSTEAD?

And the God of all grace, who called you to his eternal glory in Christ,
after you have suffered a little while, will himself restore you and make you
strong, firm and steadfast. To him be the power for ever and ever. Amen.

1 Peter 5:10–11

Faith Quest

Read Job 3:16–19
What's the secret to spiritual restoration and contentment?

Faith Trek

"Why wasn't I buried like a stillborn child, like a baby who never lives to see the light? For in death the wicked cause no trouble, and the weary are at rest" (Job 3:16–17 NLT).

While this may sound morbid, I (Arnie) once shared Job's sentiments. *Why was I ever born?* I asked myself. *Why can't I die instead?*

It was a dark period of my life. I was miserable, and no matter how hard I tried, nothing seemed to move me closer to God. In fact, the more things I attempted to do that seemed "Christian," the deader I felt inside.

Growing up, I got a ton of good thoughts and wise advice about life from some really great people: my parents, a few well-meaning folks at church, coaches, teachers. And it was, at the time, just what every child needed. But as I hit my late teens and early twenties, I started seeing chinks in the armor of leaders. Moral failures, hypocrisy, and then my own behavior started to go south, as well. The more difficult my life became, the more I prayed, asking God to save me from whatever problem

I got myself into. Yet the more I prayed, the farther away God seemed to be. And He never answered my shouts for help—or so it seemed to me.

Diving into the field of humanistic psychology, I was exposed to a plethora of ideas and actions, and suffice it to say, they didn't always match up with Jesus' take on life. I was told that "god" is in every one of us, and that if we are smart enough to break away from all of our messed-up, "religious hang-ups," we could be free as a bird. Slowly but surely in my quest for spiritual freedom, I was being sold antibiblical thoughts, with the natural corresponding antibiblical behavior following pretty closely behind—all in the name of having a free spirit—free from anything religious! Sadly, twenty-seven years later, I was so confused, I couldn't recognize spiritual truth. I ended up calling bad "good," and good "bad." My theme song was Peggy Lee's "Is That All There Is?"—"Let's keep dancing, break out the booze and have a ball!"

While it seemed fun at the time, I was empty inside.

In the midst of all of this being-free-from-religion stuff and thinking that I controlled my destiny, I occasionally got the impression that maybe everything wasn't so great in this land of "enlightened freedom." When I was thirty, for example, I completed my 5,500-square-foot dream house but still wasn't happy or fulfilled. Strangely, I became obsessed with the idea of hanging myself from a balcony off of the courtyard. Something was terribly wrong in the world I'd created for myself.

But about eighteen years ago, I launched into the process of knowing Jesus—a process that, for me, happened very slowly. And as I looked back at my old life, I began to see the irony of it all: my quest to be free and to become my own god was, in reality, turning me into a slave. I was in bondage to selfishness, pride, lust, depravity, and—though I wouldn't have labeled it this way—my own twisted sin nature.

Soon I faced a new challenge: *How do I set myself free spiritually?*

The more I thought about my past failed relationships, the more overwhelmed I became. *Loser—that's all I am and ever will be*, I'd constantly tell myself.

Eventually, one truth changed everything: *I have to win today if I'm going to win the race in all of my tomorrows.*

It sounded a bit cliché, yet it made sense. *I have to win* today. *That's all I need to focus on!* While I couldn't change yesterday (or just about anything in my past), it didn't have to define who I was, and what I did today.

Spiritual losers can get unstuck and actually become winners as they focus on today and connect with Jesus in a consistent and genuine way. Too often even devoted Christ followers forget that we have a personal, relatable, and persistent Savior who loves us deeply despite our sin and flaws—and who forgets our yesterdays and tells us not to worry about our tomorrows. Yesterday is there to be learned from, not stuck in. And the worries of tomorrow can only be released to God, not owned and clutched tightly in our hands. God owns tomorrow.[1]

Faith Tools

- Give up the perks and quirks of "Club Christianity," and strive to know the one true Christ of the Bible. Open God's Word and get started.
- "Eat up" Scripture regularly and tap into a two-way conversation with Jesus.
- **Pray**: "Lord, help me to give up empty religion and start having a thriving, growing relationship with You." Ask God to show you how to *engage* His Word, not just read it.

Notes for Growth

Key Point I Learned Today:

_____

_____

_____

How I Want to Grow:

_____

_____

_____

My Prayer List:

_____

_____

_____

Day 15

JOB'S LAMENT NO. 4: WHY WON'T THE TURMOIL END?

"What I feared has come upon me; what I dreaded has happened to me.
I have no peace, no quietness; I have no rest, but only turmoil."

Job 3:25–26

Faith Quest

Read Job 3:20–26
How has God helped you during times of turmoil?

Faith Trek

Are you among those who believe that spiritual warfare is pure fantasy—the stuff of chilling novels and thriller movies? Do you read the book of Job and shrug your shoulders. *It's a carefully crafted literary masterpiece, the work of a wisdom writer of extreme skill. It's filled with prose and poetry and other literary forms: laments, hymns, proverbs. But as for practical lessons that can be applied to the real world—well, not so much.*

Sixteen-year-old Jon, an American MK (missionary kid) living in Chaing Mai, Thailand, wants to change your mind: "The spiritual battles my family faces here are incredible," he says. His parents are Christian missionaries who work with the hill tribes of northern Thailand. "This is a perverse culture that really needs Christ," he continues. "A lot of weird stuff has been known to happen here."

Case in point: Several years back, on Kang Pan Tao hill—a sacred Buddhist site near Chiang Mai—thousands of snakes engaged in deadly duels, leaving hundreds of reptiles dead. This strange battle left many Buddhists in fear.

A Buddhist monk told the press, "In ancient times these duels would signify an enemy attack was about to take place."

It appears he was right. For several weeks in a row, hundreds of

Christian churches worldwide were praying for Buddhist countries, and nine prayer teams journeyed specifically to Thailand.

"Christians are making progress in this country—mainly with young people," Jon says. "But with more progress, comes more spiritual battle. And things are really starting to intensify here."

The mission field isn't the only battlefront. Just look around your own neighborhood—even within your home. Satan and his troops are viciously attacking the kingdom of God. His target: our souls.

But God is greater, and prayer is powerful. So, exactly how should you pray for others, as well as yourself? And what can you do to survive spiritual warfare in your own life?

Stay on guard and stand victorious for God. How? By facing reality:

First, as Job's story reveals, expect conflict—not comfort. Billy Graham describes Christians as soldiers and points out that our Captain does not promise us immunity from the hazards of battle. "Jesus told His followers that the world would hate them. They would be arrested, scourged, and brought before governors and kings. Even their loved ones would persecute them. As the world hated Him, so it would treat His servants. He also warned, 'a time is coming when anyone who kills you will think he is offering a service to God' (John 16:2)."[1]

Second, know that the enemy operates on a personal level. He seeks to lure us into a hostile position toward God and uses every kind of distraction imaginable—boredom, selfish desires, inferiority, drug abuse, doubt, fear, materialism (the list could fill up this book).

Third, know that Satan's biggest ally is our flesh itself. This is the human, physical dimension of our life that instinctively wants to live independently from God. Even though you now have a new nature in Christ, the sinful world still tempts you to return to those old ways of thinking and living (see Romans 8:5–8; Ephesians 2:3).

Faith Tools

- Remember that God has not abandoned us. In times of distress, call out to Him, and He will give you the power of the

Holy Spirit. He will help you handle whatever it is that you must face.

- We must hold tight to our hope in Jesus: "For God so loved the world that he gave his one and only Son, that whoever believes in him shall not perish but have eternal life" (John 3:16).

- **Pray**: "Jesus, everything that I've read in the book of Job has shown me that spiritual warfare is real—and that scares me." Ask the Lord to help you trust Him and to live in confidence, not in fear.

Notes for Growth

Key Point I Learned Today:

_____

_____

_____

How I Want to Grow:

_____

_____

_____

My Prayer List:

_____

_____

_____

A SUFFERER ATTRACTS "FIXERS"
THE WAY ROADKILL ATTRACTS VULTURES

"If one ventures a word with you, will you be impatient?
Yet who can keep from speaking?"

JOB 4:2 ESV

Faith Quest

Read Job 4:1–6
When is "good advice" best kept to yourself?

Faith Trek

Job's friends sat with him in silence and listened to his lament before God until Eliphaz found he could no longer hold his tongue.

He began by acknowledging the spiritual leadership Job had provided to others. We saw earlier how Job led his children, calling them to worship and offering sacrifices on their behalf. Eliphaz commended Job for teaching and encouraging many others as well.

Then the compliments became a rebuke. Eliphaz scolded Job for his reaction to his suffering. He reminded him to revere God and to hold fast to his integrity.

How do you think Job reacted to this advice? He probably wasn't too surprised. We humans are naturally curious, seeking explanations for the big and small events in our lives. Moreover, suffering brings out the temptation in us to offer advice.

In fact, these verses are just the beginning of a long section of verses in which Job's friends offer their explanations and advice for his situation. Their care and concern for Job motivated their speeches.

Good motivations, however, don't always produce good results. Instead unsolicited advice or worthless explanations may compound suffering. It can't roll back time, nor can it bring back whatever was lost.

Depending on the nature of the advice, it may also make the sufferer feel guilty for the situation. For example, well-meaning people often encourage friends struggling with depression or anxiety that God will heal them if they just have faith, trust God more, or remove any unconfessed sin in their lives. What sounds like good advice and encouragement to the adviser actually comes across as condemnation for the depressed or anxious listener.

We can learn two important lessons from these truths. First, when we are comforting someone who is hurting, we must choose our words carefully. We must be extra sensitive to how the person is feeling and how our words will sound to her or him at that moment.

When we are the ones hurting, it's important to keep in mind that sometimes even well-meaning friends may say things that deepen instead of ease the pain. Consciously choosing to let those words roll off of us rather than let them sink into our minds and spirits is the best approach.

Faith Tools

- Often friends offer unsolicited advice when trying to comfort someone who is hurting.
- The advice may be helpful or hurtful, so it must always be given with care.
- **Pray**: "Father, help me to remember to choose my words carefully when speaking with friends who are hurting. When others offer advice for my own pain, help me to remember that they do so from a kind heart." Ask God to guide your tongue and give you wisdom to know which words will comfort most.

Notes for Growth

Key Point I Learned Today:

_____

_____

_____

How I Want to Grow:

_____

_____

_____

My Prayer List:

_____

_____

_____

BEWARE—SOME PUT GOD IN A BOX

*"As I have seen, those who plow iniquity
and sow trouble reap the same."*

Job 4:8 esv

Faith Quest

Read Job 4:7–11
Is your view of God limited by your own box of beliefs?

Faith Trek

As Eliphaz continued his speech, he presented a delightfully appealing, yet woefully wrong view of the world. His words in the form of logic statements would simply be: "Good things happen to good people," and "Bad things happen to bad people."

Each of these statements is half correct. Good things do indeed happen to good people. Unfortunately, in this fallen world, bad things happen as well. Similarly, while it is true that sin produces harmful consequences, God's grace and mercy allow for good things to come to those who choose not to follow him. As we are told elsewhere in Scripture, God allows rain to fall on the just and the unjust. We also read that He wants for all to be saved and for no one to perish.

Eliphaz's words signal two spiritual dangers. First his formula condemns Job, the very man he's trying to comfort. By his reckoning, all of Job's losses are evidence that he is not as righteous as he appears.

The second danger is even greater. Eliphaz's beliefs have essentially contained God in a box, limiting Him to responding only to human behavior and to doing so with only rewards or punishments.

This box ignores the fact that God has a plan and purpose for each of us. It ignores His abundant mercy and grace. It ignores His love so great that He tests, disciplines, and molds us to be more like His Son each day.

In our day, we are blessed to be able to get to know God through His Word. Job and Eliphaz did not have such a joyous treasure. Yet even with the Bible, we may each discover times in our lives when we have put God in a box.

I (Pam) remember a time when my husband and I were trying to decide whether to move to Nebraska. With four small children, was it really wise to move to the middle of the country where we didn't know a soul and our family was so far away? We prayed about this decision for many weeks. At one point, I became almost paralyzed by uncertainty and anxiety about whether it was God's will for us to move. One day while I was praying about this decision, God reminded me that He was much bigger than our decision about whether to move. I was humbled as I realized that I had placed God in a box, thinking that God's plans and purposes hinged on our decision, and if we decided wrong, He couldn't handle it.

As you work to overcome the hurts in your own life, take some time to consider whether you have put God in a box. How will seeing God as the all-powerful Creator and Savior change you and your life?

Faith Tools

- It's tempting to believe in a just world—that good things only happen to good people and bad things only happen to bad people.
- When we ignore truths about God, we limit our relationship with him.
- **Pray**: "Lord, sometimes it's hard to remember that bad things do happen to good people in this fallen world. Help me to be sensitive to how such thoughts limit my view of You." Spend some time reflecting on how your beliefs may have put God in a box in your own life. Challenge those beliefs with truths from scripture.

Notes for Growth

Key Point I Learned Today:

_____

_____

_____

How I Want to Grow:

_____

_____

_____

My Prayer List:

_____

_____

_____

REJECT LOOSE BIBLE INTERPRETATIONS

"Now a word was brought to me stealthily;
my ear received the whisper of it."

JOB 4:12 ESV

Faith Quest

Read Job 4:12–16

How do you protect yourself from loose Bible interpretations?

Faith Trek

Today most Americans, whether they choose to follow Christ or not, have two or three Bibles in their homes. With Bible apps like YouVersion and goTandem, we have the Bible at our fingertips on our mobile devices. Moreover, after Jesus' ascension into heaven, we also have the Holy Spirit to guide and teach us.

Living in these times, it's hard to imagine a world without access to the Word. Job's world was entirely different. There was no Bible that everyone could study and discuss together.

When we consider this reality, it should not be too surprising to find that Eliphaz was offering Job spiritual advice based on his own personal experience. He talked about how the word came to him "stealthily" amid visions and dreams.

In speaking this way, Eliphaz was implying that he had special knowledge from God and so Job should treat his words as God's truth. How do you think Job took this? Hopefully not simply at face value. Because of his intimate relationship with God, Job knew God. This knowledge gave him a standard against which he could compare Eliphaz's words.

We face the same challenge today as others often tell us that "God said this" or "the Bible says that." Depending on what is going on in our lives at the time, their interpretation may be tempting. We may want to believe what they say because it seems to provide an easy answer to our problems.

Yet, just like Job, we must be cautious and discerning. People seem to have a natural tendency to overestimate their knowledge of the Bible. For example, many believe that "God helps those who help themselves" is from the Bible, when it was really penned by Benjamin Franklin in *Poor Richard's Almanac*.

Rather than taking someone else's word for it, we must search the scriptures for ourselves. We need to prayerfully discern if this new information is consistent with the biblical message. Above all, we must reject loose Bible interpretations that lead us away from God rather than to Him.

Faith Tools

- Eliphaz attempted to advise Job based on his visions and dreams, which he believed were from God. To know what God really said, we must carefully search the scriptures ourselves, rather than relying on often loose interpretations from others.
- **Pray**: "Lord, thank You for the gift of Your Word. Help me to search the scriptures for myself instead of taking the easy route of relying on someone else." Spend some time this week observing how often you engage the Bible for yourself. Would you like to make any changes?

Notes for Growth

Key Point I Learned Today:

_____

_____

_____

How I Want to Grow:

_____

_____

_____

My Prayer List:

_____

_____

_____

AVOID THE PRATTLE OF RELIGIOUS SMALL TALK

"Between morning and evening they are beaten to pieces;
they perish forever without anyone regarding it."

JOB 4:20 ESV

Faith Quest

Read Job 4:17–21
How can you avoid religious small talk?

Faith Trek

As Eliphaz described his vision, it is easy to see why it was frightening to him. He pointed out that no one is holy and able to stand before God on his or her own, a sentiment also found in Romans 3:23. Eliphaz's rendition, though, includes dramatic phrases such as "crushed like the moth" (Job 4:19 ESV) and "they perish forever without anyone regarding it" (verse 20 ESV).

A burning question is whether Eliphaz's words were helpful to Job in his suffering. If he intended his words to have an evangelistic impact, he was wasting his breath. Job already had a relationship with God.

Was Eliphaz's intention to explain Job's suffering as a punishment from God for his sins? As we've discussed earlier, such simple explanations fail to capture the full reality and put God in a box. Moreover, they could have driven Job to feel guilty about his losses.

Eliphaz's words didn't express empathy or sorrow for Job either. Nor did they build Job up by pointing him to God and a future hope.

So what useful purpose did they serve? Unfortunately, they appear to be just religious prattle—foolish or simple-minded talk. For those who are hurting, religious prattle distracts and discourages. Just as junk food provides a quick fix to hunger that ultimately fails to nourish the body, oversimplified religious chatter without a clear purpose fails to restore hope to the brokenhearted. It may stand in the way of the sufferer seeking comfort directly from God.

Avoiding religious small talk is wise advice for both those who are hurting and those who want to provide comfort. Instead, we should seek to encourage and build each other up through reminders of God's promises and future hope.

Faith Tools

- We must be careful not to slip into religious small talk when trying to comfort others.
- Our words should encourage and build each other up in the faith.
- **Pray**: "Father, help me to choose my words carefully when I'm comforting others. May my words encourage, give hope, and bring glory to You always." Spend some time studying God's promises. Note those Bible verses so they will be handy when you are encouraging someone who is hurting.

Notes for Growth

Key Point I Learned Today:

_____

_____

_____

How I Want to Grow:

_____

_____

_____

My Prayer List:

_____

_____

_____

NICE PEOPLE, NASTY ADVICE

"Watch out for false prophets. They come to you in sheep's clothing,
but inwardly they are ferocious wolves. By their fruit you will recognize them."
MATTHEW 7:15–16

Faith Quest

Read Job 5:1–7
Are you flooded with advice from friends and family? How do you know
which advice to listen to? Who's right? Who's not?

Faith Trek

Job was in pain. His entire world had been turned upside down. I (Michael) can imagine him curled up on the ground in despair. As we discussed earlier, he had lost his family, his wealth, and his health. It's just too much for one person to process. He could barely catch his breath enough to cry out in desperation. But when he did, he cursed the day he was born.

His friends, Eliphaz, Bildad, and Zophar came to visit. They didn't even recognize him at first. And when they did, they wept and tore their clothes. For the next seven days, they sat by his side in silence. They saw firsthand how tormented he was. Eliphaz, who thought of himself as a man of great experience and wisdom, reminded Job that many others had suffered in life. And now that it was Job's turn, he was not handling it well. He called him impatient and questioned his integrity. Eliphaz claimed that he had received a mystical vision from God. He implied that Job had resentment toward God and warned that this would bring more harm his way.

Bildad suggested that maybe Job's children had sinned against God and that their doom was deserved. He challenged Job to repent before

God so he could be restored to greatness. He believed that earthly blessings were a sign of one's obedience to God. And therefore Job and his family must have done something to deserve such loss and pain.

And his friend Zophar claimed that Job was guilty of wrongdoing. He reminded Job that God sees all and will not stand by and let wickedness go unpunished. He begged Job to confess in hopes of God having mercy on him. He, too, was convinced that Job had brought this suffering on himself.

Job turned to God for answers in the midst of his loss. But what he got instead were his friends. Or maybe they were just acquaintances or colleagues. They came to him in his time of need, but what they brought was just more confusion. They saw him lying there in despair and freely gave advice. But it was advice from their limited perspective and understanding. And therefore it was clouded with cultural misconceptions and agendas. Job, through his pain and questioning, remained firm that he was clean before God. But his friends kept insisting that they knew better. The heated conversation just kept circling around.

Then Elihu, a younger man, spoke out. (We'll come back to him on Day 50.) He was upset with all of them. He rebuked Job for relying on his own actions to make him clean and for questioning God. And he was angry with Eliphaz, Bildad, and Zophar for not having better answers. They continued to rebuke Job even though they could not find any reasons to justify their beliefs. In this, Elihu condemned self-righteousness while reminding them of God's great power and wisdom. Finally, God spoke to Job and reminded him that He was Job's provider. He was the one who could justify the weak and make them whole. And He was not happy with Job questioning His ways.

We all have difficult days. Sometimes we are so overwhelmed that we don't know how we got ourselves into a situation, and often we do not know how to get out of one. We seek advice from friends and family. Sometimes we read books and listen to sermons. But a better start is to begin with prayer and the Bible. Go to the source. Don't rely on someone else's interpretation of the Scriptures. Read them for yourself. With honesty and prayer, God will speak into your life and offer you peace in the midst of disappointment.[1]

Faith Tools

- Recognize that anyone giving you advice is also human and is capable of making mistakes.
- Double-check all advice with the Bible. God is consistent with His guidance.
- **Pray**: "Dear God, please help me to recognize Your ways. Please grant me clarity of mind and peace in my heart. Bring me to Your path through prayer, Your Word, and the support of Your people."

Notes for Growth

Key Point I Learned Today:

_____

_____

_____

How I Want to Grow:

_____

_____

_____

My Prayer List:

_____

_____

_____

TIP NO. 1: INSTEAD OF "QUICK FIXES" PURSUE LASTING GROWTH

"He performs wonders that cannot be fathomed,
miracles that cannot be counted."

JOB 5:9

Faith Quest

Read Job 5:8–16

Are you willing to wait patiently as you bring your requests to God?

Faith Trek

In today's passage, we find that Eliphaz told Job to appeal to God, laying his cause before Him. And he reminded his friend that the Lord's ways are good and just but that they don't always conform to human expectations. Finally, some good advice!

The book of Isaiah echoes a similar theme, quoting God this way: "'For my thoughts are not your thoughts, neither are your ways my ways,' declares the LORD. 'As the heavens are higher than the earth, so are my ways higher than your ways and my thoughts than your thoughts'" (Isaiah 55:8–9).

Yet Eliphaz was preaching to the choir. Job knew these truths all too well. In fact, the man described as "blameless and upright" had learned that as we pray and appeal to our heavenly Father, we must be prepared to wait. And that's exactly what Job was trying to do—it's just that the pain was clouding his judgment.

We can learn at least two lessons from Job's circumstances:

Sometimes, we must wait—even when it hurts. God has promised to speak to our hearts, so we can expect Him to, but He is not compelled to tell us everything we want to know the moment we desire the information. God may take His time speaking. By causing us to wait, He prepares us for His answer, which we may have missed had He spoken immediately. We have to be prepared to listen, and we must be patient as God molds our character.

As popular author Henry T. Blackaby points out, these times may draw out and stretch our faith. "[God] will take whatever time is necessary to grow your character to match His assignment for you. . . . Character building can be long and painful. It took twenty-five years before God entrusted Abraham with his first son and set in motion the establishment of the nation of Israel. Yet God was true to His Word."[1]

But at all times, we must surrender every doubt, every desire, every struggle to God. Here's what C. S. Lewis tells us about giving up control and surrendering ourselves to Jesus:

The almost impossible thing is to hand over your whole self— all your wishes and precautions—to Christ. But it is far easier than what you are trying to do instead. For what we are trying to do is remain what we call "ourselves," to keep personal happiness as our great aim in life, and yet at the same time be "good." We are all trying to let our mind and heart go their own way—centered on money or pleasure or ambition—and hoping, in spite of this, to behave honestly and chastely and humbly. And that is exactly what Christ warned us you could not do.[2]

Faith Tools

- Don't expect immediate answers.
- Let go and trust God—even when your circumstances don't make sense.
- **Pray**: "I don't always understand the difficult times I encounter— the hurt, the temptations, the trials—but I will trust You, Lord Jesus. I know that You hear my prayer and that You care." Ask God for an extra measure of strength and patience.

Notes for Growth

Key Point I Learned Today:

_____

_____

_____

How I Want to Grow:

_____

_____

_____

My Prayer List:

_____

_____

_____

TIP NO. 2: INSTEAD OF FEARING THE WORLD, FEAR THE LORD

*"But be sure to fear the LORD and serve Him faithfully with
all your heart; consider what great things he has done for you."*

1 SAMUEL 12:24

Faith Quest

Read Job 5:17–19

What's the difference between worldly fear and the fear of the Lord?

Faith Trek

Fear. It's one of those words we don't like—unless we're at an amusement park.

When we're buckled into a roller coaster, we're pretty confident that nothing worse than losing our lunch is going to happen. And we're at least somewhat certain that the ride will be over in thirty seconds, gently delivering us to that long line we waited in for thirty minutes—just to get scared!

So "amusement park fear" is acceptable because it's a mere imitation of real, raw, spine-tingling fear. This kind is actually entertaining.

The type of emotion most people connect with the word *fear* is terror: The fear of pain or damage to ourselves. Included in this definition is the fear of losing a friend or a loved one. This type of fear can generate plenty of worry, stress, and anxiety—can't it? And there's no doubt that this is the level of fear Job was experiencing.

Every day in our own lives, we experience low levels of "common-sense fear." You know, good, respect-inducing fear—the kind that tells us not to step into the street in front of that oncoming semi and to keep our fingers out of the flame. That little alarm triggers inside our heads, shouting: "Respect the consequences! Stay away from the things that can hurt or kill you!"

But let's jump back to Job's life and explore yet another kind of fear that his story illustrates. In several passages, the Bible tells us that (1) to fear God is the beginning of wisdom, (2) the fear of the Lord leads to life, and (3) the Lord delights in those who fear Him. What do you suppose is meant by this style of fear? And why are there so many scriptures that instruct us to fear God, not man?

The Lord wants to build in us the courage needed to walk boldly with Him. Charles H. Spurgeon explains it this way: "You will need the courage of a lion to pursue a course that could turn your best friend into your fiercest foe. For the sake of Jesus Christ, you must be courageous. Risking your reputation and emotions for the truth requires a degree of moral principle that only the Spirit of God can work into you. Do not turn back, do not be a coward; be a hero of the faith. Follow in your Master's steps. He walked this rough way before you."[1]

In order to give us courage and to develop strong characters in us, God wants us to have a healthy fear of the Lord—the kind that is rooted in respect and reverence for Him. But our Savior also wants to drive out worldly fear—the sort that stems from doubt and condemnation; the type that leaves its victims panicked and paralyzed and ineffective for service in God's kingdom.

To accomplish His goals, God wants us to take responsibility for our actions and to know that sin is serious business, that the fear of the Lord leads to life. One day we all will give account for our choices. This reality actually terrified Paul and motivated him to strive to please God in everything he did (see 2 Corinthians 5:9–11).

In my walk with Christ, I (Arnie) have sometimes found myself directly in harm's way. And during these moments, I've noticed three things going on inside me: I've feared for my own life, I've questioned whether I was ready to meet God, and I've felt the assurance of God's protection.

It's good to assess the condition of our hearts and, like Paul, strive to please God in everything we do. (Knowing that we'll give account for our actions is a healthy fear.) Above all, it's comforting to know that we are in the grip of His protection. Each time that I've gone up against the power of man, the power of God has overruled. *God is all-powerful and eternal.*

He protects us, nurtures our character, and drives out worldly fear.[2]

Faith Tools

- Be confident that a believer walks with the protection of our Lord Jesus Christ. And even though God calls us to bear some burdens, some hurts, and some trials, He will continue to work in us, giving us a heart like His.
- Keep in mind that our highest calling is living in respectful fear of the One who spoke the universe into being and who holds us in the palm of His loving hand.
- **Pray**: "Lord help me to have a healthy fear of You, a reverence for You and Your ways." Ask Jesus to drive out worldly fear.

Notes for Growth

Key Point I Learned Today:

_____

_____

_____

How I Want to Grow:

_____

_____

_____

My Prayer List:

_____

_____

_____

TIP NO. 3: INSTEAD OF PLATITUDES, SEEK THE TRUTH

"Are God's consolations not enough for you, words spoken gently to you? Why
has your heart carried you away, and why do your eyes flash, so that you
vent your rage against God and pour out such words from your mouth?"

JOB 15:11–13

Faith Quest

Read Job 5:20–27
Do you get mad at God during difficult times?

Faith Trek

Job was in a terrible mess. Anyone who has read this book in the Bible is easily overwhelmed by the ridiculous amount of pain and suffering he endured. He was not an evil man. He wasn't opposing God and His ways. He did not persecute God's people or try to lead them down the wrong path. He was a good man. He loved and feared God. He was fair and treated his family well. So why did God allow him to suffer? This was the exact question Job was asking. He was searching for a logical reason why his life had turned out so badly. He questioned God. And his friends weren't much help. They were trying to convince Job that he was in the wrong and must have brought this pain on himself. Job kept explaining that he had not sinned against God. But he went too far. We all know that every human is broken and has sinned. Job was not without blame. But did he really deserve to lose everything?

It's amazing how God chose to make every human unique. As long as you live, there will never be another you. But at the same time, we all have things in common. We were all created by a powerful God. We share a life together here on this earth. We have all sinned and fallen short of the glory of God. And He offers forgiveness and salvation to each one of us.

Changes come quickly sometimes. An accident takes the life of a loved one. A routine visit to the doctor brings bad news. You get called into a meeting at work to find out your position has been eliminated and you are suddenly unemployed. Or a big storm hits town and your house is greatly damaged. These things are out of our control. And we are all susceptible to them at any moment. But even in our darkest hour, God still loves us. He is continually reaching out His hand, offering us redemption and peace.

Just like Job, we tend to lash out at God, claiming that we are being treated unfairly. We list all of the things we do correctly in an attempt to convince Him that He has wronged us. We try to make God fit into our understanding of life. But we need to understand that He does not enjoy our pain. He is the One who is reaching out trying to comfort us during those horrible days. Stop trying to keep score. Instead, praise God in the midst of the pain. Admit that you need the Savior and open yourself up to God's guidance and peace.

Faith Tools

- Seek out the stories in the Bible about good people who have been wronged. Learn from their successes and mistakes.
- Accept that we live in a broken world. And then quickly remember that God is bigger than it all.
- **Pray**: "Dear God, thank You for knowing my every thought and action and for loving me anyway. Please help me to recognize the freedom and peace that You are offering me. Help me to have the courage to accept Your redemption. Thank You!"

Notes for Growth

Key Point I Learned Today:

_____

_____

_____

How I Want to Grow:

_____

_____

_____

My Prayer List:

_____

_____

_____

TIP NO. 4: INSTEAD OF THROWING A PITY PARTY, SHARE THE PAIN

"I will not leave you as orphans; I will come to you."

JOHN 14:18

Faith Quest

Read Job 6:1–30

What helps you to cope with life's troubles and challenges?

Faith Trek

"Does a wild donkey bray when it has grass, or an ox bellow when it has fodder? Is tasteless food eaten without salt, or is there flavor in the sap of the mallow?" (Job 6:5–6).

Job claimed the right to bray and bellow, since he had been wounded by God and offered "tasteless food"—in other words, poor advice—from his so-called friends.[1] All was gone in his life, and he considered his circumstances utterly hopeless. But instead of giving up or throwing a pity party, he sought the counsel of his friends. Job was genuinely searching for truth. And that's exactly why he was pleading with them to stop being so cruel.

> *"Do you mean to correct what I say, and treat my desperate words as wind? You would even cast lots for the fatherless and barter away your friend. But now be so kind as to look at me. Would I lie to your face? Relent, do not be unjust; reconsider, for my integrity is at stake. Is there any wickedness on my lips? Can my mouth not discern malice?" (Job 6:26–30).*

Job set an example for us all by taking three vital steps during trying times:

1. Finding trustworthy counsel
2. Seeking truth
3. Expressing emotions

As sadness and despair takes hold in our lives, we have a tendency to sink deeper and deeper into a pit—causing us to wonder what we've ever done to deserve any of this, questioning why God has abandoned us.

But here's what we must remember: our emotions are highly cyclical and can bounce from extremes. So when the storms of life strike, we usually feel more frustration than faith. If we've had a fight or have been rejected, we're often more consumed with anger—not the comfort of the Almighty.

What brings on the blahs in your life? And when loneliness or depression strikes, do you stay in the pit, starving your soul, or—like Job—do you search for solutions?

Faith Tools

- Remember that emotions rise and fall like a wild ride on a roller coaster. When you're lonely and depressed today, when everything seems to be going wrong and life doesn't seem to be worth living, you need to ride it out. It may not feel very good for a while, but if you ride out these emotions, you'll discover that your circumstances will change tomorrow. Your world will seem much better. Happiness will return and the depression will disappear.

- Take comfort in this truth: Jesus shares our pain. He puts Himself in your shoes and feels everything that you feel. He is the Father of "suffering with," and the God of all comfort! And when He comes beside you and offers the strength to take your next step, you learn to walk with fellow sufferers— to let their pain become your pain.

- **Pray:** "Lord, help me not to suffer alone. Give me the strength to seek the counsel of a trustworthy friend." Ask

God to bring individuals in your life who will be a "safe harbor" for you.

Notes for Growth

Key Point I Learned Today:

_____

_____

_____

How I Want to Grow:

_____

_____

_____

My Prayer List:

_____

_____

_____

GOD CAN HEAL A BITTER HEART

*"Do not mortals have hard service on earth? Are not their days like those
of hired laborers? Like a slave longing for the evening shadows, or a hired
laborer waiting to be paid, so I have been allotted months of futility,
and nights of misery have been assigned to me."*

Job 7:1–3

Faith Quest

Read Job 7:1–21

Are you ready to let God begin a sometimes painful, yet transformational, healing process within you?

Faith Trek

In Job's pain, he began to wonder if God's only interest in people was to scrutinize them unmercifully or to take quick offense at their tiniest faults. "I have not been perfect," he explained, "but what terrible sin have I committed to deserve this?" (Job 7:17–21).

The roots of bitterness were entangling Job's heart, and many today share his dilemma. Let's look at the story of a suffering young woman we know named Kathy.

Kathy's childhood was marred by abuse. Parents who abused alcohol—and her. Dark closets, nightmares, and family secrets. Her teenage years brought more of the same, yet no one knew. Her college years were different: Kathy selected a school several states away from home and felt as if she had finally escaped.

No one sent her care packages or cute cards that said, "We miss you." But that was okay. She didn't really want to hear from anyone back home. She stayed on campus on the weekends and spent winter and spring breaks at the homes of her college roommates. She tried to imagine what it would be like to have a loving family to go home to.

One day, while she was studying in the library, Kathy met a guy named Jeff. Within hours the two were planning their first date. Two weeks later, they considered themselves a couple. Throughout the next semester, everything Kathy had ever known in her life had changed dramatically. Suddenly, someone loved her and believed in her.

Jeff knew God and genuinely talked to Him on a regular basis. He prayed to Jesus about Kathy, and soon she had a desire to know the Lord, too.

If the purpose of her past was to bring her to this period in time, Kathy felt it was worth what she had gone through. So she prayed and wept tears of repentance. Jesus was now real to her. She felt the love of the Father pouring down on her.

Five years later, Jeff and Kathy were now happily married, and she had grown in God's knowledge and grace. However, even though she and Jeff had a supportive fellowship family, Kathy's relationship with her parents was completely broken. In fact, she did her best not to think about her past.

In the months that followed, Jeff and Kathy became avid hikers. During one of their treks on property Jeff had inherited, they discover a piece of paradise in the woods—and even began making plans to build a log cabin at the location.

Anxious to get started, Jeff and Kathy broke ground, slinging shovels full of dirt into a wheelbarrow. Suddenly, they encountered a problem. Jeff hit something solid with his shovel. It just wouldn't budge.

In the exact place the foundation footers were to be dug, a root of massive proportions was discovered beneath the surface. Swinging the mattock as hard as he could and striking the root with all his might, Jeff couldn't even chip it. The thing seemed to be petrified.

As Kathy watched her husband battle the root, a wave of emotion overtook her. She sat on the ground and continued to watch.

Jeff attacked the root from every angle—then discovered that the main root had a network of smaller roots that were intertwined and gnarled together underground. This is what made the ground rock solid.

Frustrated, Kathy got up and walked away. She simply couldn't give up their plans to build the cabin on this spot with the perfect view. Hiking to rock cliffs high above the valley, she pulled out a pocket Bible and began to read.

Quietly, God spoke to her: *The root is deep and it has become hard like stone. Even though it is deep and seems impossible to remove, it isn't. You can't remove it alone, but I will remove it for you if you will allow Me to.*

It was a moment Kathy would never forget. She felt the awe of God speaking intimately to her. And she knew that her Father wasn't talking about the root Jeff was trying to remove. She knew He was telling her about the petrified root in her heart. She had tried to keep the hate and lack of forgiveness hidden below the surface. Now she wanted it out of her life.

Right there on that ridge, the love of God began to melt her —and tears began to fall. She squeezed her eyes shut and continued to pray, "I can't deal with this any longer, Lord. Remove this lifelong root of pain and bitterness. Take it away from me, and in its place give me love and forgiveness. Heal me from my past. Let me love the family who hurt me. Allow them to see Your love living in me, and save them in Jesus' name."[1]

Faith Tools

- Let Jesus take you right to the very place that may be causing you to be emotionally and spiritually stuck—and allow Him to release you to grow.
- Here's what God wants from Job and from Kathy and from you—a desire for Him: " 'Love the Lord your God with all your heart and with all your soul and with all your mind and with all your strength' " (Mark 12:30).
- **Pray**: "Heavenly Father, I desire You. I don't want anything to hinder our relationship. Go deep into my heart and uproot bitterness and sin and shame." Ask Jesus to heal you step-by-step.

Notes for Growth

Key Point I Learned Today:

_____

_____

_____

How I Want to Grow:

_____

_____

_____

My Prayer List:

_____

_____

_____

TEMPTATION CAN SEEM "FRIENDLY"

"Behold, God will not reject a blameless man,
nor take the hand of evildoers."
JOB 8:20 ESV

Faith Quest

Read Job 8:1–22
If bad things will happen anyway, why still follow God?

Faith Trek

It was now Bildad's turn to speak, and he again focused on sin. Unlike Eliphaz, though, Bildad acknowledged that sometimes in this world evildoers do seem to prosper. They may have health, family, wealth, and nice houses.

The allure of an easy life tempts all of us at times. We could watch TV instead of praying. We'd rather read the latest *New York Times* than spend time in the Word. It seems easier and more comfortable to go our own way than to serve and love others as Jesus would have us.

So if temptation looks so good and bad things are going to happen anyway, why should we still follow God? Well, there's the obvious reason that He is our Creator, the Alpha and Omega, the Almighty. He is holy and worthy of all worship and praise.

He also desires a relationship with every one of us. His love seeks us out, and only through Him do we have hope of life eternal.

We choose to follow God because we know that nothing in this world is permanent. As Bildad pointed out, houses do not stand and our days on earth are merely a shadow. Relying on anything other than God makes our trust like a spiderweb.

One evening I (Pam) was returning home with my daughters. As

I was gathering things from the car, I noticed that the girls had stopped halfway on the sidewalk instead of going in the house. They turned around and shouted to me, "Spider!" In the light of the moon, I could see a web that stretched completely across the walkway. It was at least five feet high and about three feet across as it spanned from one pine tree to another. It was the biggest spiderweb I have ever seen.

As you can imagine, the spider that created the web was not petite either. It was also sitting in the dead center of the web. So we carefully picked our way around it and went inside.

By the next morning, that giant web was gone. This is the point Bildad was making. Even the friendliest temptations eventually disappoint. Our lasting hope is in the Lord and Him alone.

Faith Tools

- The temptation to turn away from God may be especially strong when we are hurting.
- Trusting the things of this world only disappoints; our only eternal hope is found in our Lord.
- **Pray**: "Lord, you told us that following You would not be easy. It's especially hard when I'm hurting and see those who don't claim your name enjoying life. Help me to keep an eternal perspective and run to you instead of running from you." Anytime you encounter temptation today, stop and talk to God about it.

Notes for Growth

Key Point I Learned Today:

_____

_____

_____

How I Want to Grow:

_____

_____

_____

My Prayer List:

_____

_____

_____

THE PRISON OF GUILT AND SHAME

"Truly I know that it is so: But how can a man be right before God?"
JOB 9:2 ESV

Faith Quest

Read Job 9:1–35
Are you trapped by guilt or shame today?

Faith Trek

Bildad's counsel had erected strong prison walls for Job. Again Job acknowledged that he was indeed sinful while God is holy. That left him stuck as he wondered how he could ever be right before God.

When the Holy Spirit speaks to our heart and we're convicted of our own sin and guilt, it can be overwhelming. This conviction shatters our self-image that we are a "good" person. The holiness of God contrasts with our actual words, thoughts, and actions. We are confronted with our sin and the gulf that it has put between us and God.

In that state, Job cried out for an arbiter between him and his holy God. His shame and guilt had overwhelmed him to the point that he didn't even believe that his Lord would answer him (verse 16). He felt trapped, unable to move forward. He couldn't just "cheer up" (verse 27). Without a way to cross that gulf, he was condemned, and everything else he did was in vain (verse 29).

Many of us can relate to the despair that Job felt. Our pain may include guilt over what we've done or failed to do. Our hurt is compounded by shame over what has happened to us.

However, we have what Job longed for: a Savior who can cross that gulf. Through His perfect sacrifice on the cross and resurrection, Jesus cleansed us from our sins and made a way for us to become children of God. Moreover, He stands at the right hand of our heavenly Father, interceding for us in our time of need.

I've (Pam) found in counseling hurting people that guilt and shame are often the biggest hurdles to healing. Some will say that they can forgive others but feel they just can't forgive themselves for the choices they made (or didn't make). Although they acknowledge that Jesus paid for all of their sins, they still feel that their actions are unforgivable.

But the problem is that God doesn't ever tell us to forgive ourselves. Instead, we are called to accept His free gift of grace and forgiveness. When we hold on to guilt even after we have confessed to God and asked for forgiveness through Jesus, we are essentially saying that our standards are higher than God's. That realization may be just the key to letting go of that self-condemnation.

We must always remember that when we become a Christ follower, we grab on to the hope that alluded Job. Jesus frees us from the prison of guilt and shame. Even in the midst of our pain, our Savior cleanses us, frees us from our past, intercedes for us, and gives us hope of blessings yet to come.

Faith Tools

- Without an arbiter, Job was trapped in a prison of shame and guilt.
- Christ followers have the arbiter Job was seeking in Jesus, our Savior and Lord.
- **Pray**: "Lord, thank You for sending Your Son to wash me of my sins. Through You I can break free from the guilt and shame of my past." Find a way today to celebrate the freedom you have in Christ.

Notes for Growth

Key Point I Learned Today:

_____

_____

_____

How I Want to Grow:

_____

_____

_____

My Prayer List:

_____

_____

_____

WHEN LIFE DISAPPOINTS

*"Why did you bring me out from the womb? Would that I
had died before any eye had seen me and were as though
I had not been, carried from the womb to the grave."*

Job 10:18–19 esv

Faith Quest

Read Job 10:1–22
How is your pain blinding you to the joys in your life?

Faith Trek

We find in Job 10 that Job continued to share his pain. His words resounded with despair and hopelessness as he pleaded with God for an answer.

He continued to acknowledge God as Creator. In verse 12, he noted that God had granted him life, steadfast love, and care.

Rather than providing comfort though, this seemed to cause Job even more pain. He didn't understand how a loving God would allow such tragedy.

Verses 18 and 19 are particularly heartbreaking as Job lamented his own birth. The pain Job was feeling now wiped out any joy he had ever experienced in his life.

God has created us with a marvelously complex mind and the ability to feel an amazing range of emotions. In the course of just a week (or sometimes a single day!), we can encounter situations that fill us with joy, anger, love, and sorrow. Over the course of a lifetime, that's a ton of memories!

Yet we don't hold all of those experiences and memories in our mind at once. Rather, they lie dormant, coming to the forefront when prompted by some type of internal or external trigger. For Job, pain disrupted this system. He couldn't remember what it was like to feel joy and saw little chance of having any more in the future.

Maybe you have tried to comfort a friend who is blinded by pain. Maybe you have been there yourself.

Just as someone who is physically blind may rely on a guide dog to help them navigate their surroundings, someone who is blinded by pain needs a guide as well. In this case, the guide is another person to come alongside and help them remember past joys, those precious memories that bring a smile and warm the heart. The guide can also assist with creating new memories, assisting the hurting one in navigating their life going forward.

Faith Tools

- Job's pain prompted him to plead with God for understanding. It also blinded him to any of the joy he had experienced in the past or that might come in the future. We can help others deal with life's disappointments by being their guide when they are blinded by pain.

- **Pray:** "Lord, sometimes the disappointments in life hurt so much I can't see beyond them. Please remove the blinders from me and help me to feel joy again." Make a list of the joys you have experienced in your life and those that are to come in the future. Keep the list handy for when you feel overwhelmed by pain.

Notes for Growth

Key Point I Learned Today:

_____

_____

_____

How I Want to Grow:

_____

_____

_____

My Prayer List:

_____

_____

_____

A HEALTHY-WEALTHY-WISE PROPOSITION

"If you prepare your heart, you will stretch out your hands toward him."
JOB 11:13 ESV

Faith Quest

Read Job 11:1–20
Can you work your way to an easy life?

Faith Trek

Zophar decided that it was his turn to speak and answer Job's lament. He returned to the idea that Job was suffering because of his sin. In fact, he went even further, stating that because of Job's guilt, Job actually deserved worse. It's hard to imagine what worse would be!

He then went on to comfort Job with the thought that no one can comprehend the ways of God. Still, Zophar contended, if Job would just become perfect, then an easy, secure life would be his.

When stated this way, Zophar's promise of health, wealth, and wisdom for those who are perfect is almost laughable. On a deeper level, it is downright depressing. The core problem rests in the fact that fallen, sinful people can't achieve perfection. This is why we need Jesus as our Savior.

Even if we acknowledge this on a cognitive level, we may still finding ourselves striving for perfection. We behave as if following the perfect nutrition and exercise plan, having a yearly physical, and getting enough sleep will mean we never get sick. Working hard, avoiding debt, and saving for a rainy day will ensure that we'll never lose our jobs and that our checkbooks will always be in the black. Sending our children to the right school, giving them the exactly correct balance of love and discipline, and taking them to the best extracurricular activities means they will grow up to make all the right choices in life.

By themselves, none of these things are really bad. They only become problematic when we start relying on them for our security. Psychologists have found that a desire for perfection can lead to depression, suicidal thoughts, and other mental health problems.

Perfectionism and the desire for a perfect life can also take our focus off of God and our relationship with Him. We may become more focused on what we do and who we are than who He is and the purpose for which He has created us. Also, when life eventually disappoints, the "perfect" world we have created collapses like a house of cards. Seeking perfection within ourselves doesn't provide a way out of pain. Instead, we are comforted when we seek out our perfect God.

Faith Tools

- The desire of health, comfort, and prosperity can fuel a perfectionistic attitude.
- Looking for perfection in ourselves is a fruitless endeavor. A better strategy for overcoming hurt is to seek out our perfect God.
- **Pray**: "Lord, sometimes I go off track and start thinking that I can live a perfect life on my own. Forgive me for looking to myself instead of to You." Ask God to reveal to you any area of your life in which you are relying on your own strength instead of His.

Notes for Growth

Key Point I Learned Today:

_____

_____

_____

How I Want to Grow:

_____

_____

_____

My Prayer List:

_____

_____

_____

THE SECRET TO WISDOM

"With God are wisdom and might; he has counsel and understanding."
JOB 12:13 ESV

Faith Quest

Read Job 12:1–25
Where do you seek wisdom?

Faith Trek

A few years ago, a scientist at the University of South Carolina calculated how much information the average person encounters in a day. He found that with the Internet, television, radio, and other sources, we are exposed each day to information equivalent to the amount found in 174 newspapers.[1] Yet information doesn't always equal wisdom and some things remain unknowable.

The secret of wisdom is Job's primary concern in this chapter. First, he chastised his friends for their words, pointing out that they had not said anything he did not already know or that really addressed his question.

He then acknowledged that true wisdom and understanding come only from God. It is only the Lord who can see the full picture and know where everyone and everything fits in His plan.

Understanding that only God had the answers for his questions could actually be freeing for Job. He knew it was futile to worry at the questions in his own mind, turning them over and over like a Rubik's cube, trying to find the answers within himself. He knew it was pointless to seek human advice from his friends, elders, or rulers.

When I (Pam) think about my own life, I see God's wisdom in His not answering my questions, or at least not immediately. One time when someone close to me died very suddenly, I did cry out and ask Him why. It didn't make sense to my human mind, and I knew only God could provide the answer. Yet he remained silent except for the comforting word that it would all make sense one day.

Many years and events later it did, and I now understand more about how that painful loss fit into God's plan and purpose. I also see that in His wisdom He did not give me that understanding before I was ready. Had I received the answer immediately, I'm sure I would have tried to argue and bargain that there was another way. In the midst of my pain, I would not have accepted any reason because I couldn't see the future.

The answer did not come until I had healed and matured enough to accept it. Now with the perspective that's only possible with the passage of time, I can see my Father's wisdom and care of me in my pain. Through trusting that He had an answer to my question, even if I didn't know what the answer was, my faith and relationship with Him grew tremendously.

Faith Tools

- Understanding that God is all wise frees us to seek the answers to our questions from only Him.
- Trusting God's wisdom in the midst of our pain helps us to heal and grow.
- **Pray**: "Heavenly Father, I know that Your thoughts are not my thoughts and Your ways are not my ways. Help me to seek wisdom only from You." Spend some time reflecting on your life. Think about those times when God's purpose and wisdom far surpassed your own.

Notes for Growth

Key Point I Learned Today:

_____

_____

_____

How I Want to Grow:

_____

_____

_____

My Prayer List:

_____

_____

_____

A WORLD BLEMISHED WITH "GRAFFITI"

*"For you write bitter things against me and
make me inherit the iniquities of my youth."*

JOB 13:26 ESV

Faith Quest

Read Job 13:1–28

Are you taking everything personally?

Faith Trek

As Job continued his response to his friends, he clearly was struggling. He again said that his conscience was clear, and he affirmed his faith in God as his only salvation.

Still Job couldn't get past the hurt and the perception that he was being punished for some wrong. As verse 26 states, he thought God was writing bitter words against him and repaying him for the sins of his youth. He thus pleaded with the Lord to reveal to him what those sins were.

Painful events often bring into focus some tough truths. Reconciling these with the damaged view of the world around us and, as we've seen with Job, with the words of well-meaning friends, presents a formidable challenge for even mature believers.

Job knew that he had sinned in the past. He knew that God is holy and righteous. He was also subject to the human tendency to believe in a just world—that bad events are punishment for sin. All of these together lead him to conclude that his livelihood and family were taken away because of some unconfessed sin.

Contrast this chapter with Job's words in Job 1:21. Satan's intent was to cause Job to stumble and turn away from God. The turmoil Job was experiencing now suggested that the pain was starting to take a spiritual toll.

How did this happen? Perhaps Job's faith had been worn down by the noise around him. As he looked at the fallen world around him, he likely saw examples that "proved" the point that sin is punished. Moreover, his friends were repeatedly telling him that he must have some unconfessed sin in his life. He now couldn't seem to help taking all of his woes personally.

What Job was missing is the assurance we have in Christ. He didn't have the promise in Hebrews 8:12 that the Lord will remember our sins no more. Even with this assurance, pain may sometimes lead us to believe the graffiti and noise around us, that our pain results from some unforgiven sin. Dwelling there, however, doesn't help us overcome the hurt. Instead, we must boldly grab hold of God's promise to us through Jesus.

Faith Tools

- Pain tests the faith of even mature believers.
- We must not let the graffiti and noise of this world make us doubt God's forgiveness.
- **Pray**: "Lord, the world keeps telling me that I'm hurting because of something I did. Please help me to discern Your voice of truth and follow it to healing." Ask God to show you how to keep his truths at the forefront of your mind and free you from the false teachings of the world.

Notes for Growth

Key Point I Learned Today:

_____

_____

_____

How I Want to Grow:

_____

_____

_____

My Prayer List:

_____

_____

_____

ADRIFT IN A SEA OF TROUBLE?

*For in this hope we were saved. But hope that is seen is no hope
at all. Who hopes for what they already have? But if we hope
for what we do not yet have, we wait for it patiently.*

ROMANS 8:24–25

Faith Quest

Read Job 14:1–22
In spite of life's troubles, are you able to put your trust in God?

Faith Trek

Job looked beyond his own troubles and turned his attention to the human condition. And his conclusions were anything but warm and fuzzy.

"Mortals born of woman, are of few days and full of trouble," Job explained. "They spring up like flowers and wither away; like fleeting shadows, they do not endure" (Job 14:1–2).

Talk about depressing!

By the end of the chapter, we find that Job's pessimism arose not from his doubts about heaven and the afterlife, but rather from what he saw as God's unwillingness to help him. His life had become a nightmare of pain and mourning, and yet the Lord seemed so distant and silent—not even offering the tiniest speck of encouragement.

So Job's conclusion should come as no surprise: "Life stinks. . .and then you die."

Is there any truth to how Job felt? Are all humans alone in their misery, helplessly adrift in a sea of trouble? The answer, of course, is a resounding *no*! Romans 8:22–25 gives us plenty to think about—*and* to hope for:

"We know that the whole creation has been groaning as in the pains of childbirth right up to the present time. Not only so, but we ourselves, who have the firstfruits of the Spirit, groan inwardly as we wait eagerly for our adoption as sons, the redemption of our bodies. For in this hope we were saved. But hope that is seen is no hope at all. Who hopes for what he already has? But if we hope for what we do not yet have, we wait for it patiently."

Let's "pause" the book of Job for a minute and "see" these verses in action.

In the next several paragraphs, we'll head out to the high seas and drop in on one of my (Michael's) favorite real-life dramas. This story takes us to the brink of disaster and reveals how faith, courage, and "hope for what is unseen" can guide us through any storm.

It's a treacherous journey, and the fleet of eleven ships is battered almost beyond repair. Even harder hit are the nerves of the crew.

"Has our captain gone mad?" yells a sailor.

"He'll end up getting us all killed," complains another.

"I say we turn around and go back!" insists a crewman.

Fear erupts on the decks. "Go back! Go back! Let's go back to the life we once knew."

But Hernán Cortés won't budge. He has amassed his battalion of 508 soldiers and 100 sailors and has set out on an important mission for the king of Spain: to explore the New World.

Cortés silences the crowd. "Gentlemen, we can't go back now. This is our destiny. We were made for this moment."

Then he reminds his men of the words he had printed on a banner: "Brothers and comrades, let us follow the sign of the Holy Cross in true faith, for under this sign we shall conquer."

It works. And soon the ships reach Mexico.

Yet Cortés doesn't rest. He knows that other storms are just on the horizon. So he quickly goes to work, disciplining his army, welding it into a cohesive force.

Then the famous conquistador does something that will be

retold again and again in the history books: he orders his men to burn the ships. By doing so, Cortés actually saves the lives of his crew. Since the ships are so weather-beaten from the journey, returning to Spain would be risky. And by that single action, Cortés commits himself and his entire force to survival through conquest. It also ensures that they will keep their eyes on the New World, not on the life they left behind.[1]

Faith Tools

- Jesus knows there will be hardships and times when we wish we could go back to "safer" ground. Remember that He is there for us. He'll help us through the tough times. He won't sit idly by, hoping we'll have the strength to withstand. He wants to provide the inner muscle it takes to combat the outer pressure we feel.

- Jesus doesn't want us to sell out for what's comfortable or go back to the old life we once knew. He's calling us to plug into His power through prayer and Bible study and to set our sights on a greater world ahead.

- **Pray**: "Lord Jesus, help me to *know* that You are with me even when I can't sense Your presence." Ask Jesus to help you trust His promises in the Bible.

Notes for Growth

Key Point I Learned Today:

_____

_____

_____

How I Want to Grow:

_____

_____

_____

My Prayer List:

_____

_____

_____

RELIGION VS. RELATIONSHIP

But God demonstrates his own love for us in this:
While we were still sinners, Christ died for us.

ROMANS 5:8

Faith Quest

Read Job 15:1–35
What are some steps you can take to grow closer to God?

Faith Trek

Poor Job. The "blameless" man of God merely wanted a listening ear and a few honest clues to help him understand why his life had become such a mess.

Instead, he got more hellfire preaching and more bad counsel—this time from Eliphaz: "If you were truly wise, would you sound so much like a windbag, belching hot air? Would you talk nonsense in the middle of a serious argument, babbling baloney? Look at you! You trivialize religion, turn spiritual conversation into empty gossip. It's your sin that taught you to talk this way. You chose an education in fraud. Your own words have exposed your guilt. It's nothing I've said—you've incriminated yourself!" (Job 15:1–6 MSG).

But Job didn't need Eliphaz's bad brand of religion. He, like every one of us, needed an intimate relationship with the one, true God of the universe. Yet men like Eliphaz, on the other hand, want to nail down the Lord and get the rules straight so they can feel secure, so they take the proverbs as absolutes.[1] The righteous prosper and the wicked suffer—that, he believed, is God's justice. So if you're suffering, as Job was, then you must be wicked. Right?[2]

Wrong. Job has shown us that bad things happen to good people, too. God loves us no matter what, not because of perfect behavior.

What's more, the Lord created us to bond relationally with Himself.

As author Doug Banister points out, "All of us are on a lifelong quest to know [God] more intimately. We must learn how to bond with Him if we are to become the people He has called us to be. The cost of failing to bond with God can be staggering: addiction, low self-confidence, depression, religiosity, burnout, and relational problems."[3]

The God of the Bible is a relational God. The three members of the Trinity—God the Father, God the Son, and God the Spirit—exist in relationship together. Jesus described their relationship as intensely intimate. Jesus said to the Father, "You are in me and I am in you" (John 17:21).

God did not create just one human being, but two. When Adam was the only person in the universe, God said, "It is not good for the man to be alone" (Genesis 2:18). Why isn't it? Was relationship with God not enough for him? Evidently not. Adam needed to be in relationship with God and in relationship with other people. This is why Jesus summed up all the teaching of Scripture in two simple commands: love God and love your neighbor. The *R* word, "relationship," is what the Good News is all about. . .restoring the relationship for which our Father originally created us.

"Relationship, or bonding, then, is at the foundation of God's nature," writes Christian psychologist Henry Cloud. "Since we are created in His likeness, relationship is our most fundamental need, the very foundation of who we are. Without relationship, without attachment to God and others, we can't be our true selves. We can't be truly human"[4]

Considering the importance of a thriving relationship that develops over time, and understanding that religious rituals and practices can't save us—as Job's friends obviously believed—I (Arnie) have been wrestling with some difficult questions about what makes someone a sincere Christian.

What about the times when I doubt. . .or the seasons when I don't feel close to God? What about the struggles I often battle?

Is Jesus saying that it's all about a perfect score? If I don't always *do the dos and avoid the don'ts, is it possible that I could miss eternity, too?*

Is God that cruel?

Absolutely not! Change does not bring about salvation. Instead, salvation produces change in our lives. And God is incredibly patient as He works it all out step-by-step.

Yet here's something that troubles me: too often when new believers exhibit no change in their lifestyles or when they revert to former lifestyles, we often refer to them as "unsanctified, carnal Christians." However, based on my research—not theology—the term *carnal Christian* appears to be useless with regard to discipleship and genuine faith.

Here's what Jesus said: "Do people pick grapes from thornbushes, or figs from thistles? Likewise, every good tree bears good fruit, but a bad tree bears bad fruit. . . . Thus, by their fruit you will recognize them" (Matthew 7:16–17, 20).

The test of true life in Christ is growth and maturation, not verbal profession. To me, this is one of the greatest lessons we are being taught in the book of Job.

Faith Tools

- Relationship makes all the difference. More specifically, relationship with the one, true God of the Bible—not *your notion* of who God is. . .but *the real God of the Bible* who loves unconditionally, who is able to heal the soul, who forgives completely. . .and who has found a way to move us from death to life.
- Consider this about the Scriptures: "There's nothing like the written Word of God for showing you the way to salvation through faith in Christ Jesus. Every part of Scripture is God-breathed and useful one way or another—showing us truth, exposing our rebellion, correcting our mistakes, training us to live God's way. Through the Word we are put together and shaped up for the tasks God has for us" (2 Timothy 3:16–17 MSG).

- **Pray**: "Lord, guard me from wrong theology. Help me to live in truth and to know You intimately." Ask Jesus to nudge you back to Him whenever you stumble.

Notes for Growth

Key Point I Learned Today:

_____

_____

_____

How I Want to Grow:

_____

_____

_____

My Prayer List:

_____

_____

_____

TRY WALKING IN MY SHOES

"Earth, do not cover my blood; may my cry never be laid to rest!
Even now my witness is in heaven; my advocate is on high.
My intercessor is my friend as my eyes pour out tears to God;
on behalf of a man he pleads with God as one pleads for a friend."

JOB 16:18–21

Faith Quest

Read Job 16:1–22

Do you believe that accepting our brokenness is the first step toward healing?

Faith Trek

Job felt as if he was wearing a big red bull's-eye on his back and was being hunted down like wild prey: "God has turned me over to the ungodly and thrown me into the clutches of the wicked. All was well with me, but he shattered me; he seized me by the neck and crushed me. He has made me his target; his archers surround me. Without pity, he pierces my kidneys and spills my gall on the ground. Again and again he bursts upon me; he rushes at me like a warrior" (Job 16:11–14).

While Job's language seems graphic—even disturbing—who can blame him? He was a broken man. The injustices inflicted on him made absolutely no sense. Yet like Abel in Genesis 4:10, he knew that his blood was innocent and that it would "cry out from the ground" after his death. Job believed that someday God would bear witness to his righteousness (vv. 18–19).

Guess what? Countless others can relate to Job's dilemma. Men, women, and children from all walks of life and from every corner of the world have felt (or eventually will feel) worn down by life's trials.

Maybe that describes your story right now.

Try to walk in my shoes, you may tell yourself. *Try feeling my pain. . . enduring the "strikes on my cheek"—the ridicule, the scorn. Try stepping into my loneliness.*

I (Michael) am convinced that *all* are broken to some degree, yet only a few are willing to admit it. We wear masks and act as if we're okay—that we have it all together; doing so makes us feel better about ourselves and more attractive to others. But inside we're broken. And that's okay. At least that's what a friend is teaching me. Allow me to share his story.

I know this guy in Seattle who sings everywhere—coffeehouses, schools, music festivals, churches—anywhere he can draw a crowd. His voice has that gritty edge, and his songs churn up all kinds of emotions in those who listen. They make you think. Even cry.

His beat-up, twelve-string guitar looks like a yard-sale reject: It's covered with surfing stickers, duct tape, and "graffiti" from friends (notes, doodles, and autographs). Amazingly, though, he manages to pull incredible beauty out of something so ugly.

This guy is talented, yet—like his guitar—his life is pretty messy.

It started out that way.

His mom and dad abandoned him when he was a small boy, pawning him off on his grandparents. Just out of diapers and barely able to talk, his young heart was already torn and bruised. He actually started believing that he was so unlovable, so flawed, that his parents couldn't stand to be around him. And when they ended up getting a divorce, he blamed himself for that, too. Slowly a toxic mix of shame, self-loathing, and rage began to bubble inside.

Things got messier through the years, mostly because of alcohol and drug abuse during his teen years. He plunged deep into the Rastafari movement as a young man, searching for meaning to his life, but he ended up becoming more confused (not to mention really, really high all the time). He hit rock bottom at age twenty-four and spent time behind bars for using and dealing drugs.

And then he met Jesus.

After that, everything began to fall in place. . .right? He did a "Christian 180," and now he had the promise of living happily ever after.

Not exactly.

Despite ten years of "trying to get things right," his life is still pretty messy.

He reads his Bible, he prays, he devours every spiritual growth book he can get his hands on, he serves in church, he hangs out with Christ-following friends—he does all kinds of "Christian things" that Christians are supposed to do, and yet he still slips on life's messes and falls flat on his face.

In fact, he's even dealing with some new twists to a bunch of old problems: *abandonment* (this time by his wife), *divorce* (this time his own), and *imprisonment* (this time his emotions). As for that toxic shame thing, it's still pooling and swirling inside. On some occasions, usually during weak moments, it gets the best of him. Old habits and negative ways of thinking seem to take over. . .and before he realizes it, he has lost the day spiritually.

Here's what's changed during his decade of walking with Jesus: he doesn't try to hide his mess. He's actually pretty open about it, and he even writes songs about the things that trip him up. This brings out a sigh of relief in some believers who have heard his story: *I'm not alone!* they tell themselves. *I can stop pretending that I have it all together, and I can start living with authenticity just like this guy. I don't have to be afraid anymore. I can take a step toward God. . .warts and all.*

Others, though, write off his life as yet another "depressing Seattle story," and even label him *hypocritical, phony, backslidden.*

I'm with the first group.

Even though my hang-ups are different from his, the fact is, I still get hung up from time to time. I'm a Christ follower, yet I, too, don't have it all together. I'm a Christ follower, yet. . .

I have a messy faith and a messy life.

I fall flat on my face—more often than I care to admit.

I desperately need a Savior.

The truth is, we're all like this guy—and we all feel like Job from time to time.

Faith Tools

- When we accept that all are broken, we can put away all the junk that gets in the way—our efforts to "get things right" and to "do Christian things". . .our pride, our stubborn wills, our attempts to control everything and everyone.
- Jesus wants you to stop worrying about life. Let Him take care of the things that trouble you. He will correct the injustices in our lives (Matthew 6:25–34).
- **Pray**: "Lord, help me to come clean with You and to stop trying to hide my pain." Ask Jesus to go deep into your heart and to bring about lasting change.

Notes for Growth

Key Point I Learned Today:

_____

_____

_____

How I Want to Grow:

_____

_____

_____

My Prayer List:

_____

_____

_____

DON'T KICK ME WHEN I'M DOWN

Some faced jeers and flogging, and even chains and imprisonment.
They were put to death by stoning; they were sawed in two; they were
killed by the sword. They went about in sheepskins and goatskins,
destitute, persecuted and mistreated—the world was not worthy of them.
They wandered in deserts and mountains, living in caves and in holes in
the ground. These were all commended for their faith, yet none of them
received what had been promised, since God had planned something better
for us so that only together with us would they be made perfect.

HEBREWS 11:36–40

Faith Quest

Read Job 17:1–16
Can anything good come from our pain?

Faith Trek

As Job has shown us, sometimes the only way God can bless us is by breaking us. It's not easy, and it's not fun. We feel alone, wrestling and questioning, feeling empty and full of doubts—not aware that we might, in fact, be very close to an amazing encounter with God.

At times, that's how God gets our attention. When everything's going great, we usually don't hear Him very well. Yet when it feels as if we're wandering through a spiritual desert—when we struggle—He has our undivided attention. C. S. Lewis put it this way: "God whispers in our pleasure, but He shouts in our pain."[1]

Could you be on the verge of some incredible new stage of spiritual growth in your life? Or are you just sick of suffering? Maybe you're mad at God because those who don't claim Christianity seem to be having more fun than you.

It's definitely hard to accept and most certainly unpleasant to think about. But, like it or not, even good Christians suffer from time to time.

Why? "When the light comes the darkness must depart," explained Charles H. Spurgeon. "Where truth is, the lie must flee. If the lie remains, there will be a severe conflict, because truth cannot and will not lower its standard. If you follow Christ, all the hounds of the world will yelp at your heels."[2]

Living on the side of truth means struggle: saying *no* when everyone else is saying *yes*, or *yes* when they're saying *no*; holding back anger when you want to lash out; being honest when you know a little bit of dishonesty could make life easier.

When it feels as if the Christian life involves more pain and problems than blessing and bliss, consider this: It's better to endure temporary struggle, which leads to eternal joy, than momentary comfort, which results in everlasting torment.

Faith Tools

- Suffering never gets as nasty as hell (Luke 16:24). What are you suffering? A relationship gone south because you've gone religious? A boss who verbally abuses "Bible thumpers"? How about a case of cancer that won't go away? Whether your pain is short term or long, it *will* end. Even if your suffering lasts all your earthly life, heaven's welcome mat will read NO TEARS.[3]

- Suffering brings Jesus close (Philippians 3:10). In suffering for Him, you'll appreciate His great sufferings for you. And in your every struggle, He suffers with you. What's more, He gives you the strength to endure: "For the grace of God has appeared that offers salvation to all people. It teaches us to say 'No' to ungodliness and worldly passions, and to live self-controlled, upright and godly lives in this present age, while we wait for the blessed hope—the glorious appearing of our great God and Savior, Jesus Christ, who gave himself for us to redeem us from wickedness and to purify for himself a people that are his very own, eager to do what is good" (Titus 2:11–14).

- **Pray**: "Lord, help me to grow closer to You. Sometimes I feel so wearied by my struggles. Give me the strength to endure." Ask Jesus to give you an eternal focus.

Notes for Growth

Key Point I Learned Today:

_____

_____

_____

How I Want to Grow:

_____

_____

_____

My Prayer List:

_____

_____

_____

A SNAPSHOT OF DESPAIR

*No one who hopes in you will ever be put to shame, but shame will come
on those who are treacherous without cause. Show me your ways, LORD,
teach me your paths. Guide me in your truth and teach me, for you are
God my Savior, and my hope is in you all day long. Remember, LORD,
your great mercy and love, for they are from of old.*

PSALM 25:3–6

Faith Quest

Read Job 18:1–21
What helps you to drive out hopelessness during troubled times?

Faith Trek

Misery. Despair. Darkness. Sin. Bildad now returned to the themes of
his first speech, describing despair in graphic detail. He insisted that all
suffering is the result of sin, and he seemed to prattle on endlessly about
some of the ways the wicked are punished.

And as expected, Bildad's advice continued to embitter Job. (More
on that tomorrow.) But since we're on such a depressing subject, let's
look at the antidote—the ultimate Source of hope for the hopeless.

Flip back to Genesis 3 and you'll find the beginning of misery—
and hope. The story moves from sin and evil to shame and cover-up,
broken fellowship, erected barriers, attack on God, flight from God.
It's the story of the fall, out of which C. S. Lewis says "has come nearly
all that we call human history—money, poverty, ambition, war, prosti-
tution, classes, empire, slavery—the long terrible story of man trying to
find something other than God that will make him happy."

Yet the story of the fall is also one of grace—God's grace—and
hope. It's the hope that began when God broke our unholy alliance with

the devil and put hostility between him and us. Misery is still with us. But the time is getting shorter and the hope is getting brighter.[1]

Do these truths give you hope?

Take a moment to turn your attention to Jerusalem—an ancient city that is literally the "crossroads of life." It's the place where you can walk in the footsteps of Jesus and, at the same time, witness a chaotic culture that's torn apart by political and religious disagreements. It's a place of extreme joy—and misery.

As you soak in Israel's many sights, you can't help being reminded of an awesome truth: while the glory of this world is fleeting and flawed by strife, true fulfillment can be found by knowing intimately, loving intensely, serving passionately, and trusting completely Jesus Christ. Eternal peace is at the core of God's gift of salvation.

Just as it's written in the book of Acts, Jesus will return to the Holy Land—the same place where He went up into heaven. A restored Israel is very close to the heart of God. It's not only the restoration of a people to a land—but all people to their God. This is where misery ends and true fulfillment is found. This is what we all should be seeking.

Faith Tools

- Strive to choose hope—even in the midst of misery. After all, Christ died, defeating the power of death! And Christ rose. The grave couldn't keep Him down. And neither can the grave hold "those who have fallen asleep in him" (1 Thessalonians 4:14).

- Don't look to the world for true fulfillment. Instead, look to God. Isn't it ironic that the "Holy Land" is one of the most chaotic regions of the world? Understand this: strong forces, based on ancient religious beliefs are at work in the Arab-Israeli struggle. Yet there is hope even today for the troubled Middle East, as well as the entire world. Every one of Abraham's children—Arab, Jew, and Gentile alike—has the same opportunity to receive God's gift of eternal life offered in His chosen Messiah.

- **Pray:** "Please restore my hope in You, Lord Jesus—especially during those times when all I see is misery and all I feel is despair." Ask Jesus to send you the encouragement you need right when you need it most.

Notes for Growth

Key Point I Learned Today:

_____

_____

_____

How I Want to Grow:

_____

_____

_____

My Prayer List:

_____

_____

_____

ALL IS GONE—EXCEPT GOD

"For I know that my redeemer lives,
and in the end he will stand on the earth."
JOB 19:25

Faith Quest

Read Job 19:1–29
How does knowing God is always with you provide comfort when others abandon you?

Faith Trek

Other than a brief glimpse of Job's wife and his three friends, we haven't really heard much about how others responded to his tragedies. Did the neighbors band together to retrieve his children's bodies so they could have a proper burial? Did they hold a fund-raiser to help Job and his wife recover financially? Did they stop by to express their sympathy?

Job now revealed that the reality was far different. Everyone—friends, neighbors, servants, spouse and siblings—abandoned him in his time of need.

Pain and suffering can drive people away from us. They may fear that what has happened to us will spread to them. Perhaps they are afraid to see us in pain, not sure how they will be able to handle their own emotions or provide any comfort.

Truthfully, some do not care enough to be present in our suffering. With his wealth and social status, Job likely attracted more than his share of this latter type, people who wanted to be close to his power yet didn't really care about him as a person.

Whatever the reason, seeing others turn away only adds to our hurt. It deprives us of the important comforts of knowing that others care and that we are not alone.

Job looked around and saw no one standing with him except his God. He confidently proclaimed that his Redeemer lives and that He will stand on the earth.

Job's faith is inspiring. It stems from a more profound place than a simple feeling. Job knows this truth in the deepest part of his spirit, and he gained this knowledge through a close, longstanding relationship with his Creator.

As believers, we boldly make the same proclamation. Jesus has told us that He will be with us always, even to the end of the age (see Matthew 28:20). When we are our lowest and feel like the whole world has turned their backs on us, our Lord is there. What great comfort that truth provides!

Faith Tools

- Some people will turn away from you when you are hurting. The reasons vary but often have little to do with you.
- Even when friends and family walk away, your Redeemer remains with you.
- **Pray**: "Gracious Lord, thank You for being an ever-present help in times of trouble." Ask God to heal the hurt you have from the abandonment of others.

Notes for Growth

Key Point I Learned Today:

_____

_____

_____

How I Want to Grow:

_____

_____

_____

My Prayer List:

_____

_____

_____

NEVER CONTENT, ALWAYS WANTING

*"Because he knew no contentment in his belly,
he will not let anything in which he delights escape him."*

JOB 20:20 ESV

Faith Quest

Read Job 20:1–29
Is discontentment pulling you down?

Faith Trek

Zophar now took a turn, returning to the idea that eventually the godless will suffer. He honed in specifically on discontentment and how that drives people to focus on the temporary things of this world instead of the eternal.

Recently several of our Back to the Bible staff traveled to the Philippines to work with ultrapoor families alongside our ministry partner International Care Ministries (ICM). The families we ministered to live on less than fifty cents a day. We visited their homes, mostly small bamboo structures with dirt floors, patchy roofs, and little to no furnishings. They had no running water or electricity. The kitchen area was simply a few pots just outside the door.

The living conditions were indeed heartbreaking. What stood out in my (Pam's) mind most, however, was the people. Putting myself in their circumstances, I imagine I would be depressed and worried. I'm afraid I would focus so much on what I didn't have that I'd miss what I did have.

The people we met, however, were genuinely joyful. They warmly welcomed us into their community. As the women participated in classes about health and container gardening, they shared smiles, hugs, and laughter. One of my favorite memories was walking down the street with two women. The weather was sweltering of course. As we joked about the sun and heat, one of the women put her arms around our shoulders, teasing that we should carry her back to her house. What a joyful moment connecting with these beautiful women I had met only a few hours earlier.

I don't want to paint a false picture. The families had tremendous needs. I'm sure they also have their moments of worry and sadness. What humbled me, though, was that they didn't focus on what they lacked. This contrasts sharply with the picture Zophar paints in verses 20 to 23. It also contrasts with how many of us live our lives. We pour much of our energy into acquiring things and experiences we believe will make us content.

But true contentment doesn't come from the outside. It stems from our relationship with God and his forming us to become more like Christ. Through Jesus, we can replace our discontentment with the contentment Paul describes in Philippians 4:11–13 (ESV): "Not that I am speaking of being in need, for I have learned in whatever situation I am to be content. I know how to be brought low, and I know how to abound. In any and every circumstance, I have learned the secret of facing plenty and hunger, abundance and need. I can do all things through him who strengthens me."

Faith Tools

- Discontentment drags us down and diverts our energies to things that are here today and gone tomorrow.
- True contentment comes from inside as the Holy Spirit transforms us to be more like Jesus.
- **Pray**: "Father, sometimes it seems that I'm always wanting more and never content. Please help me to throw off the discontentment that is pulling me down and fully grasp the wonderful peace You have provided through Your Son, Jesus." Pay extra close attention to your language today as you go

about your activities. Do your words convey contentment or discontentment?

Notes for Growth

Key Point I Learned Today:

_____

_____

_____

How I Want to Grow:

_____

_____

_____

My Prayer List:

_____

_____

_____

MAKING SENSE OF THE SENSELESS

"One dies in his full vigor, being wholly at ease and secure,
his pails full of milk and the marrow of his bones moist.
Another dies in bitterness of soul, never having tasted of prosperity.
They lie down alike in the dust, and the worms cover them."

Job 21:23–26 ESV

Faith Quest

Read Job 21:1–34
Where do you turn when you can't make sense of the world?

Faith Trek

We're at the halfway point in the book of Job now. Despite all of their going back and forth, Job and his friends seemed no closer to explaining why we suffer in this world. Job's friends kept insisting that suffering is punishment for wickedness. Job responded with examples of the godless prospering and the righteous experiencing tragedy. How were they going to make sense out of all of this?

So far they had tried to reason using human logic, religious small talk, and anecdotes. None of this had sufficed. They had no way of knowing what had occurred in the spiritual realm between Satan and God.

They were also limited to this point in time. They did not know what would happen in the future. Sometimes short-term suffering leads to a long-term gain. Consider, for example, the life of Joseph. He was sold into slavery when he was seventeen years old. He made his way up in Potiphar's house, and then unjust accusations from Potiphar's wife condemned him to prison.

Scripture tells us that Joseph continued to follow God during this time. Still, being human, Joseph had to wonder why these things were happening to him.

Years later when Joseph was in a position to save not only his family but many others from famine, he realized how God's plan had enfolded. He made that wonderful statement to his brothers: "As for you, you meant evil against me, but God meant it for good, to bring it about that many people should be kept alive, as they are today" (Genesis 50:20 ESV).

What if Job and his friends could never get to that point; what if they could never make sense of the senseless? What then? This is a critical question, because the seemingly nonsensical things in this world block many people from following God. They simply can't reconcile a loving and merciful God with the pain and brutality around them.

Sometimes, like Joseph, we discover later that what appeared senseless actually had a place in God's plan. Other times no explanation comes and we have to rely on our faith that God is still in control.

Faith Tools

- Human logic, anecdotes, and the limitations of time are little help in making sense out of the senseless.
- We rely on our faith and trust in God most when we are plagued by "why" questions.
- **Pray**: "Lord, I see much senseless suffering when I look at the world around me. I rely on You to get me past the 'why' questions that plague me." Spend some time considering the pain you are feeling. What will help you heal even if you're never able to make sense of the pain?

Notes for Growth

Key Point I Learned Today:

_____

_____

_____

How I Want to Grow:

_____

_____

_____

My Prayer List:

_____

_____

_____

WHEN WE ARE FALSELY ACCUSED

With his mouth the godless man would destroy his neighbor,
but by knowledge the righteous are delivered.

PROVERBS 11:9 ESV

Faith Quest

Read Job 22:1–30

How should a Christ follower respond to false accusations?

Faith Trek

Eliphaz decided it was time to give Job some "tough love" by pointing out how great his wickedness was. He was not talking in generalities this time but made several specific allegations. Eliphaz contended that Job had stolen from the poor, failed to give sustenance to the thirsty and hungry, turned away widows, and crushed orphans.

We can only imagine that these allegations pierced Job's soul. He was a man who feared God and shunned evil. Because of his long relationship with the Lord, his heart was likely softened toward widows and orphans, who hold a special place in God's heart. Just the thought that he had hurt them likely angered and offended him.

It's certainly understandable that Job was angry. Letting that anger dictate his response to Eliphaz would not help matters. Anger produces hurtful words, further escalating the situation as our adrenaline rises. As Solomon wrote, "A fool gives full vent to his spirit, but a wise man quietly holds it back" (Proverbs 29:11 ESV).

Job could have gotten defensive, pointing out all of the good things he had done. The problem is that Eliphaz had already reached his conclusion—that Job failed to take care of the poor. Job in essence would have to prove a negative—that he did not fail to do something. That's a nearly impossible task.

So how would Job navigate the pain from this salt Eliphaz had rubbed in his wounds? He didn't have to show up to the argument Eliphaz had invited him to attend. He could simply not respond directly to Eliphaz at all. Instead, he could rest in the assurance that his heart was right before God. And he could trust that his Lord would answer the accusations for him.

Jesus faced many accusations during His earthly ministry. At times, He addressed them directly (see, for example, Matthew 12:9–14). Other times He did not. When He was arrested and brought before Pilate, the elders brought many charges against Him. We read in Mark 15:3–5 (ESV): "And the chief priests accused him of many things. And Pilate again asked him, 'Have you no answer to make? See how many charges they bring against you.' But Jesus made no further answer, so that Pilate was amazed."

In the moment, when our ears are searing from the harsh words against us, the pain and adrenaline urge us to respond quickly and decisively. Most of the time such a response only makes matters worse. We are wise to remember what Proverbs 11:9 (ESV) says: "By knowledge the righteous are delivered." The false accusations may never be proven false this side of heaven and our accusers may always hold their negative opinions of us. Ultimately, though, it is not human opinion that matters.

Faith Tools

- False accusations from others can compound our pain.
- When we feel attacked, we must slow down and carefully choose a response that honors God. Often that will be no response at all.
- **Pray:** "Lord, the words of others pierce my heart when they falsely accuse. Help me to follow Jesus' example in how I respond. May I always remember that it's my relationship with You that truly matters." Ask the Lord for His strength and wisdom when responding to false accusations.

Notes for Growth

Key Point I Learned Today:

_____

_____

_____

How I Want to Grow:

_____

_____

_____

My Prayer List:

_____

_____

_____

WHEN WE FEEL ABANDONED

"But he knows the way that I take;
when he has tried me, I shall come out as gold."

JOB 23:10 ESV

Faith Quest

Read Job 23:1–17
How do you know God is still there when you can't "feel" Him?

Faith Trek

In Job 23, we see Job struggling with his feeling that God had completely abandoned him. His words reflect the depths of his despair as he wondered where God was when he needed Him most.

Most Christ followers can relate to Job's situation. In our research, we've found that Christians feel spiritually stuck or far from God about three months out of the year. The problem is so common that we (Arnie and Mike) wrote an entire book on the subject called *Unstuck: Your Life. God's Design. Real Change.*[1]

What's interesting about Job's lament is that it contains rays of hope amid the pain. He acknowledged that he felt bitter, that he was groaning in despair, and that he couldn't perceive God's presence. Still he knew that God is all powerful and that after this trial he would "come out as gold."

Job's struggle appears to have stemmed from a conflict between his knowledge of God and his emotions. While our emotional experiences are real and can't just be dismissed, they are not a solid foundation on which to base our faith. Feelings are fleeting and can arise from a variety of physical, cognitive, and situational factors. They give color and flavor to life, such as the excitement of meeting a new challenge or the joy of holding a newborn baby.

We get into problems, though, when our faith in God depends on our feelings. Factors such as exhaustion, pain, or even feelings of guilt may block our ability to sense God's presence. At those times, we must intentionally remind ourselves that our faith rests securely on Christ. We know this by returning again to our knowledge of God and the truths we find in His Word. We can look back over our lives and recall our heavenly Father was with us then, even if we didn't feel it at the time.

This is the time to seek out the strength and encouragement of other believers as well. They help us to keep walking through our current darkness and into the light. Like Job, we must choose to continue to pursue God despite our momentary feelings.

Faith Tools

- Most Christ followers experience times when they are spiritually stuck and feel far from God's presence.
- When we're stuck, we must remind ourselves that feelings are not the foundation of our faith.
- **Pray**: "Father, I rejoice in your presence today. Please help me to remember that You are always with me even when I feel abandoned." Ask the Lord to open your eyes to those around you who are feeling spiritually stuck. Intentionally pursue ways to encourage them in their faith.

Notes for Growth

Key Point I Learned Today:

_____

_____

_____

How I Want to Grow:

_____

_____

My Prayer List:

_____

_____

_____

THE ILLUSION OF SECURITY

They may be allowed to live in security, but God is always
watching them. And though they are great now, in a moment
they will be gone like all others, cut off like heads of grain.

JOB 24:23–24 NLT

Faith Quest

Read Job 24:1–25

How do you keep from being discouraged when evil goes unpunished?

Faith Trek

Nearly everyone, no matter what his or her religion, agrees that there is evil in this world. Some acts of evil, from the Holocaust to the killing fields of Cambodia to the genocide in Darfur, are so extensive and shocking that they produce a public outcry and become a major part of history. Countless other evil acts are against individuals, causing physical, psychological, and spiritual damage.

Healing the wounds in the aftermath of these evil acts becomes all the more difficult when it seems that the evildoer has "gotten away with it." The pain they have caused appears to have no effect on them at all. In fact, by all accounts, they are content and secure, not concerned in the least with the consequences of their actions.

Job reminds us that the security of the evildoer is in fact a delusion. Ultimately the evildoer will face the consequences of choosing not to follow God.

Remembering that actions in this world have consequences in the next provides comfort for believers. It does not, however, excuse us from fighting for the poor, oppressed, and victimized now. As Christ followers, we are Jesus' hands and feet on earth. We are to speak for the voiceless and seek justice for the oppressed (see, for example, Proverbs 31:8–9; Isaiah 1:17).

Advances in communication and technology provide more tools than ever for these tasks. Through the media, Internet, and watch groups such as Open Doors USA, we can learn what is happening in other parts of the world, pray for those affected, and urge authorities to take action. Closer to home, we can get involved in a variety of advocacy groups that help the poor, orphans, or victims of violence.

Actions such as these show others that we care for them and so does our Father in heaven. As we focus on helping others, we are helped to overcome our own pain. It helps us to actively wait for the Lord, remembering that He will one day put to right all that is wrong. As Psalm 37:10–11 (ESV) says, "In just a little while, the wicked will be no more; though you look carefully at his place, he will not be there. But the meek shall inherit the land and delight themselves in abundant peace."

Faith Tools

- Healing is difficult when evildoers seem secure in their evil.
- As Christ followers, we know their security is illusive and God ultimately will right the wrongs.
- **Pray**: "Lord, thank You for Your love, mercy, and healing. Help me to remember that the world I see around me is not all there is." Seek the Lord's will on how He is calling you to give voice to the voiceless and to help the poor and oppressed.

Notes for Growth

Key Point I Learned Today:

_____

_____

_____

How I Want to Grow:

_____

_____

_____

My Prayer List:

_____

_____

_____

THE MYTH OF PERFECTION

"How then can man be in the right before God?
How can he who is born of woman be pure?"

JOB 25:4 ESV

Faith Quest

Read Job 25:1–6
How will accepting yourself as you are help you overcome your hurt?

Faith Trek

In just a few short lines, Bildad captures one of the most important spiritual truths: humans are by nature sinful, and on our own, we can't stand in the right before God.

The idea that we can work our way to righteousness is a dangerous one. It sets us on an endless treadmill of trying to be pure in our own power and then failing miserably. Failure produces guilt that we can't, on our own, remove. The myth that perfection is possible keeps us on edge, always nervous that we will slip up. And then when we do, we're plummeted to the depths of despair.

What joy we have today in knowing that we can bust the myth of perfection because God extends His grace to us through His perfect Son. He lived the perfect life we never can, and through the salvation He provides, we are reconciled to God. His Holy Spirit fills our hearts and over time transforms us to be more like Jesus each day.

At the end of this section, Bildad concludes that because we can't achieve holy perfection, we are the same as maggots and worms. Ah, this is a lie Satan would love for you to believe. If you believe that you are lower than the worms, you will run from God, instead of running to Him. You will keep quiet about your faith instead of boldly proclaiming it.

At the core, the myth of perfection assumes that God's grace is dependent on you. The awesome news is that it is not! God's grace is a free gift!

We must always remember that while it's a free gift to us, it came at the enormous price of Jesus' death on the cross. God does indeed love us so much that He was willing to sacrifice His own Son so that we may have fellowship with Him. What a sharp contrast to Bildad's contention that we are no better than worms!

When Satan is whispering such lies in our ears, we need to stop and give ourselves a reality check. We cast off the myth of perfection and boldly declare that we are God's precious child.

Faith Tools

- The myth of perfection assumes God's grace depends on us and traps us in a cycle of anxiety and guilt.
- We must never forget that God's grace is a free gift through Jesus.
- **Pray**: "Lord, your love overwhelms me. Thank You for sending Jesus to die for me." Commit to memorize scripture about God's love and grace that you can use to combat the myth of perfection. In addition to John 3:16–17, consider Ephesians 2:4–5, 8–9 and Romans 5:1–2.

Notes for Growth

Key Point I Learned Today:

_____

_____

_____

How I Want to Grow:

_____

_____

_____

My Prayer List:

_____

_____

_____

Day 44

HELP FOR THE HELPLESS

*"Behold, these are but the outskirts of his ways, and how small a whisper
do we hear of him! But the thunder of his power who can understand?"*

JOB 26:14 ESV

Faith Quest

Read Job 26:1–14
What help will you boldly ask God for?

Faith Trek

Helplessness qualifies as one of the world's most frustrating emotions.
Anyone who has spent hours trying to console a crying baby understands what it's like to feel that there's nothing he or she can do to
improve a situation.

Maybe you're feeling helpless today because you're out of work and
have no job offers, despite all of your applications. Maybe you have an
autistic child and are struggling with understanding and communicat-
ing with him. Perhaps your spouse is suffering from depression and you
don't know how to help her.

Job recalled that God helps those who have no power and saves
those who have no strength. He then spent time considering God's
majesty. He talked about the Lord's creative power and control of the
natural world, including the wind, water, and creatures.

Jesus displayed this power as well in His earthly ministry. Consider the thirty-seven miracles documented in the Gospels, including
turning water to wine; feeding thousands; calming a storm; walking on
water; healing the blind, lame, sick, and demon-possessed; and raising
the dead to life.

One of my (Pam's) favorite accounts is of the woman in Mark 5
who suffered from uncontrollable bleeding for years. What helplessness
she must have felt as she went to physician after physician, only to find

the problem getting worse. She didn't let that helplessness cripple her. She took the risk to touch Jesus' robe and experienced the miracle of healing.

Contrast this with the phenomenon of learned helplessness, when we give up trying because of consistent failure. Years of psychology research shows that anytime we feel stuck in a bad situation, we're at risk of surrendering to our helplessness, and thus we can miss when escape is possible.

Our world today looks very different from biblical times. But our God is the same. He still has the same power and remains our help in times of trouble. Job shows us that we need to focus on God's majesty and power most when we are at our weakest.

Faith Tools

- Difficult situations can wear us down and can convince us that we can't do anything to make things better.
- Focusing on God's majesty and past miracles soothes feelings of helplessness.
- **Pray**: "God, I am awed by Your majesty and power. Today I boldly ask for Your help in the challenges I am facing." Make a concerted effort to watch carefully for how God is working in your life and the lives of your loved ones. Be alert to the opportunities He opens for you to change your circumstances.

Notes for Growth

Key Point I Learned Today:

_____

_____

_____

How I Want to Grow:

_____

_____

_____

My Prayer List:

_____

_____

_____

HOPE FOR THE HOPELESS

"Remember not the former things, nor consider the things of old.
Behold, I am doing a new thing; now it springs forth, do you not perceive
it? I will make a way in the wilderness and rivers in the desert."

ISAIAH 43:18–19 ESV

Faith Quest

Read Job 27:1–23
What are you looking forward to most?

Faith Trek

As we're making our way through the book of Job, we're getting an inside look at Job's changing emotions. Sometimes he was deep in his grief, mourning the tragedies that had occurred. Other times he was angry, lamenting why these things had happened when he'd been so faithful to God.

And sometimes he was hopeful, declaring that he knew his Redeemer lived. At the darkest moments, the promise that things will change and the situation will get better keeps us going. It gives us a reason to wake up in the morning, get dressed, and face the day.

What did Job have to hope in? His children and his servants were not coming back. The sheep and cattle, too, were gone forever. If Job's hope rested solely on everything returning to exactly as it was before, he hoped in vain.

One of the most impactful experiences I've (Pam) had in my professional life is working on a crisis hotline. Though it was also referred to as a suicide hotline, most of our callers were not contemplating taking their own lives. Rather, they were struggling with some issue such as grief, depression, post-traumatic stress, or loneliness. Each call was different, depending on the caller's needs. However, after we had talked them through the crisis, we would ask them what they planned to do next. This wasn't a strategy to end the call so we could move on to the next. It was a deliberate technique to get them to look forward to something with anticipation. As we sat in a tiny, poorly furnished room answering calls from desperate people, we tried, in our own small ways, to instill some hope in their lives.

Job pointed out that we have no hope beyond this life if we do not follow God. For him, hope remained. He still had a loving God whom he trusted, even when he was in pain and asking questions. Because of his hope, Job boldly proclaimed that he would hold on to his integrity.

Romans 5:3–5 also talks about hope: "We rejoice in our sufferings, knowing that suffering produces endurance, and endurance produces character, and character produces hope, and hope does not put us to shame, because God's love has been poured into our hearts through the Holy Spirit who has been given to us."

Did you catch the "produces" part? It means that we aren't just given a certain allotment of hope when we're born and that's all we have. It grows as we endure life's trials and let the Holy Spirit work in our hearts.

Faith Tools

- If you choose not to follow God, you have no hope beyond this life.
- Hope grows as we continue to trust the Lord through life's trials.
- **Pray**: "Father, thank You for the hope You've given me for eternal life with You. Help me to face each day with endurance and abundant hope." Make a list of all the things you have to look forward to, from the small to the large, from what's happening tomorrow to what's in the world to come.

Notes for Growth

Key Point I Learned Today:

_____

_____

_____

How I Want to Grow:

_____

_____

_____

My Prayer List:

_____

_____

_____

WALKING IN WISDOM

*"And he said to man, 'Behold, the fear of the Lord, that is wisdom,
and to turn away from evil is understanding.'"*

Job 28:28 esv

Faith Quest

Read Job 28:1–28
What wisdom have you gained from following God?

Faith Trek

When people talk about Job, they typically emphasize his patience and endurance. But he was also a wise man. He may not have had all of the answers to life's big and little questions, but he did know where wisdom could be found.

Many of us love to seek out advice before making a decision or choice. The first "agony aunt" advice column appeared in the *Athenian Mercury* in 1690. A group of experts answered reader questions, ranging from philosophy to science. In the United States, the syndicated "Dear Abby" column became an icon of popular culture, answering thousands of letters over several decades. Today magazines, newspapers, and the Internet offer a plethora of advisers ready and willing to answer any burning question you may have. Online ratings and reviews also give you quick "wisdom" from total strangers about how well various products and services worked for them.

Seeking advice from someone who is wiser about a particular topic is often a sound approach. Our allergist has much more knowledge and experience with asthma than I (Pam) do, so I rely on her wisdom in managing my daughter's condition. My mechanic knows which type of oil will keep my old car running best.

In these examples, the advisers have specific experience and knowledge related to the issue. At other times, advice may be forthcoming, but it doesn't stem from wisdom. Consider the folly of King Rehoboam in 1 Kings 12. He received radically different advice from his friends and his father's advisers. He decided to go with his friends' wisdom, leading to a split in the kingdom of Israel.

In a more modern example, columnist Ann Landers offended the USA Rice Federation in 1996 by stating that the tradition of throwing rice at weddings was harmful to birds, causing them to explode when they ate it.[1] The truth is that there are good reasons not to throw rice, but exploding birds is not one of them.

Job reminds us that ultimate wisdom concerning the great questions of life can't be found in the land of the living, among people or among the natural world. He affirms that true wisdom is only found in our Creator. And when we walk in the ways of God, turning away from evil and asking God for help, He will share His wisdom with us (James 1:5).

Faith Tools

- Job's wisdom in responding to his troubles stemmed from knowing that true wisdom comes from God.
- We grow in wisdom when we walk in the ways of God.
- **Pray**: "Lord, You tell us in Your Word that You will generously give us wisdom when we ask. I'm asking today to be filled with wisdom for the challenges I face." Spend some time seeking what God's Word has to say about a problem you are facing. Be alert for new insights into how you should respond.

Notes for Growth

Key Point I Learned Today:

_____

_____

_____

How I Want to Grow:

_____

_____

_____

My Prayer List:

_____

_____

_____

BETTER DAYS WILL RETURN

*The steadfast love of the LORD never ceases; his mercies never come
to an end; they are new every morning; great is your faithfulness.*
LAMENTATIONS 3:22–23 ESV

Faith Quest

Read Job 29.1–25
Describe God's faithfulness through the storms of your life. Did better
days return?

Faith Trek

In this chapter, we hear directly from Job about how wonderful his life
was before Satan asked to test him. He paints the picture of a perfect
life. He was bathed in God's friendship, surrounded by his children, able
to be generous with the poor, and respected by the entire community.

When I (Pam) was in high school, Bruce Springsteen's song *Glory
Days* was at the height of its popularity. The song chronicles the experiences of a grown man as he meets up with various high school pals. He's
struck by how they all keeping referring back to their "glory days" when
they were in high school.

I remember as a high school sophomore singing along to this song,
imagining all of the joyous events that lay ahead of me. My perspective
was quite different when I heard the song again just a couple of weeks
ago, more than twenty years later. This time I found it bittersweet. Yes, I
have many fond memories of my high school friends and adventures. I'd
be pretty sad, though, if my memories ended there.

Job's recollection of his previous life brought a similar reaction. His
memories may have been sweet to him, like looking through a scrap-
book of family memories is to us. But Job wasn't going to get stuck

there, and he couldn't see his current situation as the end. He still had better days ahead.

King David, who also experienced his share of highs and lows in life, penned Psalm 30 at the time he dedicated the ground on which his son would build a temple to the Lord. Imagine him recalling the exhilaration of being told he was going to be king, of defeating Goliath, and of ultimately becoming one of the greatest rulers of Israel. Mixed in were the painful times of Saul trying to kill him, his fall into sin with Bathsheba, the death of his son, and the fighting among his children. In the psalm, he looks back over his life and confidently declares that God's favor lasts a lifetime and, though weeping may last throughout the night, rejoicing comes in the morning.

Recounting our good memories can provide comfort in tough times. It reminds us of the wonders God has performed in times past. Amid this remembering, we can't forget that God has promised that better days lie ahead, too.

Faith Tools

- Our memories of the way life used to be can provide comfort in times of pain.
- We must be careful not to get locked in the past. We must always remember that God's faithfulness is great and better days are ahead.
- **Pray**: "God, great indeed is Your faithfulness. Help me to live in joyful anticipation of the better days ahead." As you reflect on the ups and downs in your life, think about how God has demonstrated His faithfulness.

Notes for Growth

Key Point I Learned Today:

_____

_____

_____

How I Want to Grow:

_____

_____

_____

My Prayer List:

_____

_____

_____

Day 48

WHAT DID I DO TO DESERVE THIS?

*"Surely no one lays a hand on a broken man when he cries
for help in his distress. Have I not wept for those in trouble?
Has not my soul grieved for the poor? Yet when I hoped for good,
evil came; when I looked for light, then came darkness."*

Job 30:24–26

Faith Quest

Read Job 30:1–31
How do you handle circumstances that seem unjust?

Faith Trek

Does it ever seem like you just can't catch a break? You look around and
see other people enjoying life while you muddle through. We all have
challenges, but some people seem to come out better off while you just
keep running into a wall. You work hard. You try to be a good person.
You pray and go to church. But you can't seem to break the chain of
misfortune. You probably don't have any illusions of grandeur. You just
want enough space to breathe. It would be nice to have one paycheck
that isn't spent before you deposit it. You long for good friends who
accept you even on the bad days. But they don't seem to be found. You
wish for a car that starts every morning without the assistance of jumper
cables. You're looking for a life partner who is true and honest. But you
just keep dating jerks that use and abuse you. And in the middle of it all,
you manage to smile and put on a good face. You joke about how crazy
life is and proclaim that you are a survivor. But deep down inside you
are lonely and depressed.

Stop comparing yourself to others. That's right. We all fall into the
trap of sizing up our lives by comparing them with the lives of those

around us. Did it ever cross your mind that maybe those people, too, are putting on a good face? Yes, some people seem to have a lot of good fortune. But most people would admit that life is hard. We are so caught up in looking to others to gauge how we are doing in life, we miss the point of life. This may sound cliché, but we should be looking to God instead. The accomplishments of this world are only lasting if they fall within the will of God. And His ways are so often completely different from the world's. He has a master plan and wants to include you and me. He is powerful and protective. He wants us to focus on Him and on loving one another. Life is not about getting ahead or getting the recognition of those around us. It's about discovering the life-changing ways of the Lord and pursuing them with all our hearts. The more we seek God, the more we will recognize that money, fame, and earthly success can be empty pursuits. If it's not rooted in Christ, then it's not worth our time. The good news is, He wants us to have good relationships and honorable work. And living a life focused on God's ways will open us up to a peace and happiness that only God can give.

So stop trying to live up to someone else's expectations. Turn your attention to God and study His ways. He wants to help you. He has given us prayer, the Bible, insightful teachers, and a long tradition of practices that can bring us closer to Him. Seek them out and invest your energy in these things. God is waiting for you.[1]

Faith Tools

- Make a list of your dreams that coincide with God's ways.
- Intentionally do one thing a day that helps you focus on God's love for you.
- **Pray**: "Dear Father, thank You for all You have done for me. Please help me to see You more clearly as I go through my day. Please help me to recognize Your hand in my life as I draw closer to You. Thank You!"

Notes for Growth

Key Point I Learned Today:

_____

_____

_____

How I Want to Grow:

_____

_____

_____

My Prayer List:

_____

_____

_____

THE UGLY CONSEQUENCES OF SIN

Indeed, there is no one on earth who is righteous,
no one who does what is right and never sins.

ECCLESIASTES 7:20

Faith Quest

Read Job 31:1–40
What does it mean to be holy?

Faith Trek

"Does [God] not see my ways and count my every step?" Job asked. "If I have walked with falsehood or my foot has hurried after deceit—let God weigh me in honest scales and he will know that I am blameless—if my steps have turned from the path, if my heart has been led by my eyes, or if my hands have been defiled, then may others eat what I have sown, and may my crops be uprooted" (Job 31:5–8).

Job was blameless and upright; he feared God and shunned evil (Job 1:1). While he was aware that he wasn't immune to sin—no person is—he took seriously the ugly consequences of disobedience and made every effort to walk in holiness. So in this climactic section of speeches, Job listed several possible sins that he knew he had not committed, and then he attested to his loyalty to God as his sovereign Lord.

He began with the sins of the heart—especially sexual lust and marital infidelity—and moved into many other ills that plague humanity: cheating in business, dishonesty, social injustice, lacking compassion for those in need, ignoring widows and the fatherless, covetous greed, idolatry, and hypocrisy.

Job didn't try to sugarcoat an otherwise unpleasant topic. In fact, he set the tone for a frank discussion about sin and holiness that is relevant to modern-day Christians.

Because sin separates us from God, and since the Bible says that all who place hope Christ "purify themselves, just as he is pure" (see 1 John 3:3), unholy living isn't even an option for the Lord's people. In other words, Jesus destroyed the "sin license" and gives those who follow Him a new desire (essentially, a brand-new heart) that enables them to be righteous "just as he is righteous" (1 John 3:7; see 3:5–10).

A Kansas City pastor, and a ministry friend of Back to the Bible, picks up where Job left off. He beautifully sums up a universal truth we all should take to heart:

> *A relationship in close communication with Jesus is the only way to live. As we abide in Him, he lives through us. [This relationship] is dynamic, real, and personal. It is an invitation to a holy "highway" of living. Jesus had an intimate relationship with the Father and He intends for us to know that we can be one in and with Him. [This] is the great invitation to be a holy people, not in our efforts, abilities, or energies, but in a death to self, so that He might live in us moment by moment. Without Him in this moment, nothing but darkness remains.[1]*

Holy living is central to the life of a Christian. Being real through and through is one of the most important characteristics of God's people—something we must model to the world. And consider this: God sees every action and hears every word we speak—even those uttered from lying lips. Though we may be able to deceive others, we simply cannot lie to God—not now, not ever.

Our heavenly Father is quick to offer forgiveness when we ask for it. He understands our humanity, which is why He looks favorably on those who—like Job—strive to walk in obedience and holiness.

Faith Tools

- Steer clear of phony faith. It isn't hard to miss: we say one thing then act another way; we find faults in others but overlook our own; we call ourselves Christian but catch ourselves acting like the world.
- Desire integrity and be comforted, not fearful, by the fact that the Lord keeps us in His sight. He will guide our steps and guard our lips if we let Him. What does integrity look like? Share this

list with your friends, family, and members of your church:

- Integrity understands that all of life is on display before God (1 Kings 9:4).
- Integrity serves as a guide in life's moral decisions (Proverbs 11:3).
- Integrity hates falsehood in every form (Proverbs 13:5–6).
- Integrity is something to be held on to, even in tough times (Job 2:3).
- Integrity keeps its word even when to do so hurts (Psalm 15:1–4).
- Integrity backs up what it says with how it lives (Titus 2:7).
- **Pray**: "Lord, help me to seek honesty at the deepest levels. I know all too well how easy it is to bend the truth from time to time, stretching the facts to make something sound better. Help me to avoid doing this." Ask the Lord to give you a passion for holiness.

Notes for Growth

Key Point I Learned Today:

_____

_____

_____

How I Want to Grow:

_____

_____

_____

My Prayer List:

_____

_____

_____

Day 50

CONSIDER THE SOURCE

"Turn to me and be saved, all you ends of the earth; for I am God, and there is
no other. By myself I have sworn, my mouth has uttered in all integrity a word
that will not be revoked: Before me every knee will bow; by me every tongue will
swear. They will say of me, 'In the LORD alone are deliverance and strength.' "
All who have raged against him will come to him and be put to shame.

ISAIAH 45:22–24

Faith Quest

Read Job 32:1–22
What does it mean to rage against God? (Are you guilty of doing this?)

Faith Trek

Job's three friends now fell silent.

They were talked out, stymied because Job wouldn't budge an
inch—wouldn't admit to an ounce of guilt (see Job 32:1 MSG). But at
that moment, another man spoke up, offering his two cents' worth. His
name was Elihu, and he was a brash young guy who tried to put the
others in their places and solve the mystery of Job's problems.[1] He was
the son of Barakel the Buzite (of the family of Ram), and like the others
who had come to console Job, Elihu brought more harm than healing.

"Do you three have nothing else to say?" Elihu asked, losing his
temper. "Of course you don't! You're total frauds! Why should I wait any
longer, now that you're stopped dead in your tracks? I'm ready to speak
my piece. That's right! It's my turn—and it's about time! I've got a lot to
say, and I'm bursting to say it" (see Job 32:15–18 MSG).

Exactly what were Elihu's "words of wisdom" that he couldn't wait
to impart? We'll find out in tomorrow's devotional. But for now, let's
leave the conversation and ponder some truths we can bank on: insights

from Isaiah, son of Amoz and a man who is thought of as the greatest of the writing prophets.

Reread Isaiah 45:22–24 (above) and consider this: Job, you, and I (Michael) are God's beloved, and He is our Strength, our Deliverer. We carry the mark of His Son who has sought us at a great price and who has placed on us great value. We are the jewels set in His crown. Our lives matter to Him.

Now that's the advice I'd give someone in Job's shoes.

Even though life doesn't make sense sometimes and people let us down, God can be trusted. Through Jesus, God has betrothed Himself to us. "I will betroth you to me forever; I will betroth you in righteousness and justice, in love and compassion" (Hosea 2:19). He does not change like the wind, and He will never leave us or forsake us (see Deuteronomy 31:6).

The One who loves us speaks wisdom to our spirit and leads us in the way we should go. Regardless of what path our feet may be on, His voice is constantly speaking (whether we listen or not), saying, "This is the way; walk in it" (Isaiah 30:21).

The Lord *will* lead us out of the storms.[2]

Faith Tools

- If we disconnect ourselves from God's Word, we can fall into darkness. We cannot know the will of God—and the way out of darkness—if we do not become intimately acquainted with Scripture.
- The situations we encounter that stir up ugly emotions may not change, but we can possess a peace that surpasses human understanding. There's a peace in the core of our being because we have trusted God to be our Warrior, Provider, and Deliverer.
- **Pray**: "Jesus, draw me close to You. You're all I want. Help me know You are near." Ask God for wisdom. Ask Him to help you handle hard times.

Notes for Growth

Key Point I Learned Today:

_____

_____

_____

How I Want to Grow:

_____

_____

_____

My Prayer List:

_____

_____

_____

TEMPTED TO THINK GOD DOESN'T CARE

In you, LORD, I have taken refuge; let me never be put to shame. In your righteousness, rescue me and deliver me; turn your ear to me and save me. Be my rock of refuge, to which I can always go; give the command to save me, for you are my rock and my fortress. Deliver me, my God, from the hand of the wicked, from the grasp of those who are evil and cruel.

PSALM 71:1–4

Faith Quest

Read Job 33:1–33
In what ways is God your rock and your fortress?

Faith Trek

Elihu spoke passionately to Job. He was thoroughly convinced that he had something life-changing to impart—and that he had solved the mystery of Job's unfortunate circumstances.

"Look, I'm human—no better than you," the young man told Job. "We're both made of the same kind of mud. So let's work this through together; don't let my aggressiveness overwhelm you" (see Job 33:6–7 MSG).

Elihu quoted Job's own words (somewhat loosely) and then attempted to show his friend where he had gone wrong. The young man was offended by Job's claim of being pure in heart and having done nothing to deserve his lot. Just as his peers suggested, Elihu was convinced that Job must be corrected. He was committed to the traditional wisdom theology that sin causes suffering; therefore all suffering is the result of sin.[1]

"You said, 'I'm pure—I've done nothing wrong. Believe me, I'm clean—my conscience is clear. But God keeps picking on me; he treats me like I'm his enemy. He's thrown me in jail; he keeps me under constant surveillance.' " Elihu repeated what Job said earlier, and then he threw a "verbal punch" at his friend: "But let me tell you, Job, you're wrong, dead wrong! God is far greater than any human. So how dare you haul him into court, and then complain that he won't answer your charges? God always answers, one way or another, even when people don't recognize his presence" (see Job 33:8–14 MSG).

While Elihu made some accurate claims about God, he himself was dead wrong about Job. What's more, his theology was way off base. Compare his accusation with what theologian A. W. Tozer once wrote: "No man is worthy to succeed until he is willing to fail."[2] Often the moments in life that truly mold our character are those filled with struggles, flops, and fumbles—not perfect behavior and shining spiritual triumphs. The keys to survival—and ultimately success—are faith and surrender.

Tozer explained it this way: "God may allow His servant to succeed when He has disciplined him to a point where he does not need to succeed to be happy. The man who is elated by success and cast down by failure is still a carnal man. At best his fruit will have a worm in it."[3] In other words, our attitude counts. We must maintain a heart that is faithful to God regardless of our circumstances.

Turn to the book of Judges for snapshot after snapshot of raw, un-censored suffering and failure—and God's gracious, divine deliverance. "Then the Israelites did evil in the eyes of the LORD and served the Baals" (2:11). Keep reading through chapter 2 and you discover that, despite humankind's gross unfaithfulness, *God is faithful*. He molds and disciplines His children. He shows persistent, unwearied love and matchless grace; grace that's absolutely underserved. "Then the LORD raised up judges, who saved them out of the hands of these raiders" (v. 16).

In God's perfect time, He gives a new beginning to people who so easily turn their backs on Him; rebellious children who break promises; generations that know more than a little about failure—people like you and me.

Faith Tools

- Don't be paralyzed by life's struggles and mishaps. The Lord wants to transform tremendously flawed individuals into heroes who are fit to accomplish His purposes. Don't let life's blunders get in the way. Instead, *let God have His way*.

- The next time you face a really bad day, consider this: God created you, which means you are a valuable, one-of-a-kind masterpiece. The Bible says you are "fearfully and wonderfully made" (see Psalm 139:13–16). God—the creator of the universe, the master of all He surveys, huger than huge and older than ancient—knows you personally and says you matter to Him.
- **Pray**: "Lord Jesus, I really need You to protect me from the humiliation the world is dishing out right now. Please turn my sorrow into joy." Ask Jesus to help you understand how "wildly" He loves you. Ask Him to help you believe that He loves you no matter what.

Notes for Growth

Key Point I Learned Today:

_____

_____

_____

How I Want to Grow:

_____

_____

_____

My Prayer List:

_____

_____

_____

TEMPTED TO BLAME

*Therefore, hear me, you men of understanding: far be it from God that he
should do wickedness, and from the Almighty that he should do wrong.*

JOB 34:10 ESV

Faith Quest

Read Job 34:1–37
Have you ever blamed God or people for your circumstances?

Faith Trek

We love to find someone or something to blame for our problems. The
first account of sin in the Bible also includes the first round of the blame
game. According to Eve, it was all the serpent's fault. Adam contended
that God was responsible because God created Eve.

It's no surprise that we have inherited the tendency to blame, along
with Adam's sin nature. When bad things happen, we feel a loss of control, so identifying someone as the cause of what happened helps us
regain that sense of control.

Emerging science links our propensity to assign blame to a particular area of the brain (the temporoparietal junction) that is involved
in moral decision making. When we blame, we place ourselves in the
position to judge who is morally responsible.

Bildad, Eliphaz, and Zophar declared that Job was morally responsible for his problems. They blamed the victim for his pain, something
that is common today, especially in cases of bullying and sexual assault.

Elihu took a different angle because he recognized that Job's present troubles were tempting him to blame God. He pointed out that Job
was partially correct: he had not done anything wrong. His words, however, were those of a wicked man, for he attributed his troubles to God.

With strong words, Elihu reminded Job that our Lord is holy
and can never be wicked. Job's accusatory words say as much, rather
than placing the blame on Satan and his evil schemes. These words

create great spiritual danger.

Our English word *blame* actually derives from the Latin *blaspheme*. Elihu's words certainly make that connection when the temptation is to blame God. He reminded Job and the other friends that there is no wickedness in the Lord and He can't do wrong. God allowed Satan to test Job, but He did not take Job's children, livelihood, and health. In the same way, God allows pain in our own lives to strengthen our faith and to draw us closer to Him.

Faith Tools

- We have a natural tendency to assign blame for the troubles in our lives.
- We are on spiritually dangerous ground when we blame God.
- **Pray** : "Lord, help me to always remember that You are holy and there is no wickedness in You." How will accepting that God has allowed pain in your life help you to overcome it?

Notes for Growth

Key Point I Learned Today:

_____

_____

_____

How I Want to Grow:

_____

_____

_____

My Prayer List:

_____

_____

_____

TEMPTED TO STOP BELIEVING

I believe that I shall look upon the goodness of the LORD
in the land of the living! Wait for the LORD; be strong,
and let your heart take courage; wait for the LORD!

PSALM 27:13–14 ESV

Faith Quest

Read Job 35:1–16

Why do you continue to follow God?

Faith Trek

Take a moment to flip back to the first two chapters of Job. What was Satan's intent in testing Job? Oh yeah, he wanted to push Job so much that he would turn away from God.

The truth is that tragic events and pain in our life can shake our faith to the core and drive us to question whether we should continue to believe. Although Job's initial reaction was to bless the name of the Lord, his grief had worn him down to the point he was now questioning whether it had been worth following God when it hadn't save him from such pain.

Karen Jensen Salisbury, a Christian writer and speaker, can relate to Job's faith struggle. In 1997 her thirty-seven-year-old husband, Brent, died suddenly in his sleep, leaving her to raise their two teenage sons and to pastor their Idaho church.

In writing about this sad time in her life, she acknowledges that she had lots of hard, ugly questions for God. She didn't stop there, though. She writes: "Throughout this trying time in my life, I learned it's what we do after we ask our questions that determines what's going to happen next in our lives. So here's what I did. After I asked all my hard, scary, ugly questions, I pushed them to the back burner of my life and kept on "cooking" with God on the front burners." She kept trusting God through the valley of shadows instead of camping there with the pain.

Elihu pointed out to Job and his friends the foolishness of turning away from God in hard times. He reminded them that, despite all of their back and forth about sin and punishment, the truth is that the Lord does not depend on our behavior. Job wouldn't be punishing God if he stopped believing in Him, but he would be punishing himself. He would cut himself off from the Creator, the Alpha and the Omega.

In our day, as in Job's, most people are indifferent to God in the good times. Yet they cry out to Him for rescue when troubles come. And when the trouble passes or answers don't come fast enough, they turn away again.

Our Lord does want us to come to Him with our burdens and pain (see Psalm 55:22; 1 Peter 5:7). He also wants a relationship with us in the good times, too. That's what many of us are missing.

Elihu's words challenge us to seek God at all times and to keep believing, even in the midst of our pain and confusion. The testimony of other believers like Karen Jensen Salisbury show us the way as they put their questions on the back burner and kept engaging with God through prayer and His Word.[1]

Faith Tools

- God is not dependent on people's behavior.
- Giving in to the temptation to stop believing God is like cutting off your nose to spite your face.
- **Pray**: "Father, forgive me for the times I've ignored my relationship with You. Help me to start anew today and continue to follow You despite the hurts." Spend some time reading a biography of someone you admire. Take special note of the tough times that person faced and how he or she responded to them. Did the person stay in the valley of hurt or find a way to move on?

Notes for Growth

Key Point I Learned Today:

_____

_____

_____

How I Want to Grow:

_____

_____

_____

My Prayer List:

_____

_____

_____

LEARNING FROM OUR SUFFERING

"To me this is like the days of Noah, when I swore that the waters of Noah would never again cover the earth. So now I have sworn not to be angry with you, never to rebuke you again. Though the mountains be shaken and the hills be removed, yet my unfailing love for you will not be shaken nor my covenant of peace be removed," says the LORD, who has compassion on you.
ISAIAH 54:9–10

Faith Quest

Read Job 36:1–33
How have you experienced God's compassion in your life?

Faith Trek

Compassion is a nice word. It makes us think of random acts of kindness and sweet little ladies. We are all taught that compassion is a good thing and we should strive to show it to others. But what does it mean when we say that God has compassion on us?

Compassion can be hard. It is a willingness to give to others what they do not deserve. Have you heard the saying "Walk a mile in another man's shoes"? This isn't just another old-timey saying. It is a way of life. Imagine looking at those around us with the eyes of compassion. All of a sudden that mean store cashier has a story. Maybe she just got bad news from the doctor and is carrying the weight of the world on her shoulders. It could be that the angry guy who cut you off on the exit ramp is stressed out. Maybe he had a flat tire and is late for work. He could be afraid of losing his job and not being able to feed his family. He could be afraid of losing his job and not being able to feed his family. This perspective takes the focus off of us and places it on others. Our thoughts can become focused on the well-being of the people around us. And this can prompt us to help them—or at least give them a break.

Now image what it means for God to have compassion on us. He is the Creator of the universe who designed us each to be unique individuals. He is all knowing and powerful. And the Scriptures clearly describe

Him as a compassionate God who cares for His people. He knows our pain and heartbreak. He sees us making bad decisions and having to live with the consequences. And He chooses to have compassion. He reaches into our lives and comforts us. He made a supreme sacrifice to offer us all salvation. We can come to Him because of His love for us. The relationship can be mended. And there is no better news on earth.[1]

Faith Tools

- Thank God for the things you don't deserve.
- Strive to have the eyes of God when it comes to your interactions with others.
- **Pray**: "Thank You, God, for loving me. I know I don't deserve Your love and forgiveness. But I am very thankful that You have shown me compassion. Please help me to see others with Your eyes."

Notes for Growth

Key Point I Learned Today:

_____

_____

_____

How I Want to Grow:

_____

_____

_____

My Prayer List:

_____

_____

_____

MAN SHOWS PITY, GOD SHOWS UNDERSTANDING

*"Hear this, O Job; stop and consider the wondrous works
of God. Do you know how God lays his command upon
them and causes the lightning of his cloud to shine?"*

JOB 37:14–15 ESV

Faith Quest

Read Job 37:1–24
Would you rather have pity or understanding?

Faith Trek

In Job 37 we find that Elihu encouraged Job to consider God's majesty. He spoke of the Lord's awesome power, justice, and abundant righteousness. He reminded Job that the One who created this world understood what Job was going through.

Hearing of another's tragedy, we experience sadness, sympathy, and sometimes even pity. Aristotle asserted that to feel pity we must have some amount of distance between us and the hurting person. Although pity originally meant feelings of sorrow or sadness, its connotation today also reflects an air of superiority or condescension. Findings from neurological studies are consistent with this connotation, suggesting that pity arrives from an initial aversion to the sufferer's situation. Our mind then moves on to take in more of the context and we begin to feel empathy.

God's response to our pain goes deeper than pity. He understands our hurts. We see this in the life of the prophet Elijah. In 1 Kings 19 we see Elijah running from Jezebel, who has vowed to kill him. Disheartened, discouraged, and exhausted, Elijah cries out to God and then falls asleep under a tree. He is awakened by an angel who provides him food and water. Elijah drinks, eats, and falls asleep again. The second this messenger of God awakes him, he speaks these touching words that show God understands Elijah's plight: "Arise and eat, for the journey is too great for you" (1 Kings 19:7 ESV).

After this display of understanding, God then demonstrates His power and majesty to Elijah with a great wind, earthquake, and fire. Yet He speaks to Elijah not through these, but in a low whisper.

Just as Elijah witnessed God's awesome power and understanding, Elihu encouraged Job to do so in his time of need. He provides a wonderful reminder that our God is bigger than we can even imagine, and in Him we can find understanding.

Faith Tools

- People often respond to suffering with pity.
- Because our God is all knowing and all powerful, we can rejoice that He understands our pain.
- **Pray**: "Lord, help me experience today the understanding You showed to Elijah when he was struggling." Spend some time today worshipping and praising God. Pray that your spirit will be sensitive to hear His soft whispers to you.

Notes for Growth

Key Point I Learned Today:

_____

_____

_____

How I Want to Grow:

_____

_____

_____

My Prayer List:

_____

_____

_____

GOD SPEAKS THROUGH STORMS

Then the LORD answered Job out of the whirlwind and said:
"Who is this that darkens counsel by words without knowledge?"
JOB 38:1–2 ESV

Faith Quest

Read Job 38:1–41
What is God saying to you today?

Faith Trek

After all of the back-and-forth with Job and his friends, we now come to what Job had been waiting for. The Lord spoke to him out of the whirlwind, cutting through his pain.

One of our favorite questions to ask people is how God speaks to them. We know that He speaks to us through His Word, something that Job didn't have. He also speaks to us through the storms in our lives, the events that force us to look beyond ourselves for help and answers.

In my sixty-plus years on this earth, I (Arnie) have faced my share of losses and storms. It was through an incredible literal storm off the coast of Alaska that I came to faith in Jesus. In a boat surrounded by gigantic rogue waves, I found that when you are face-to-face with God's awesome power, you can't deny Him.

I've learned since then that when any kind of storm comes along I need to be on extra-high alert for God's voice—and for Satan's attempts to distract me.

In speaking to Job, God reoriented Job's attention. He reminded Job that Job was not God, Job's logic and reasoning would only take him so far, and Job didn't have all the answers.

God was not saying these things to belittle Job or to make him feel that he was worthless. Rather, God was gently reminding Job that

He knows the unknowable and, through their relationship, He would provide for all of Job's needs.

We don't know if Job heard God's voice audibly as Elijah and Paul experienced. At times, the Holy Spirit speaks directly to our spirits through a particular verse when we are engaged in His Word, through a sermon or teaching we hear, or through the encouragement of a friend. Regardless of the method, we know that, like Job, we have been longing to hear God speak, and God will not disappoint us.

Faith Tools

- Difficult situations can wear us down and can convince us that we can't do anything to make things better.
- Focusing on God's majesty and past miracles soothes feelings of helplessness.
- **Pray**: "Lord, thank You for using the storms in my life to speak to me." Ask God to help you discern His voice amid the noise around you. Take time to thank Him for speaking to you through your pain.

Notes for Growth

Key Point I Learned Today:

_____

_____

_____

How I Want to Grow:

_____

_____

_____

My Prayer List:

_____

_____

_____

WHEN THE LORD CONFRONTS, TAKE NOTICE

Create in me a clean heart, O God, and renew a right spirit within me.
PSALM 51:10 ESV

Faith Quest

Read Job 39:1–30
How do you respond when the Lord confronts you?

Faith Trek

As God continued speaking to Job, He didn't give direct answers to Job's questions. Rather, He asked Job a long and varied list of questions about animal behavior and the natural cycles of life.

We researchers love questions and ask them constantly. Pondering good questions forces us to think long and deep about a topic. They can force us to challenge our own assumptions and to seek the best answers.

In this instance, the questions served another purpose. They were confronting Job with the fact that there was only one God. . .and that God wasn't Job.

Committing our lives to Christ sets us on the path to becoming more like Him. Through praying, engaging scripture, having account-ability, and navigating our way through life's trials, God transforms and molds us into the image of Jesus.

Growing in Christ is a process and takes time. Inevitably we hit bumps in the road, times when we go off track and respond with our sinful human nature.

Thankfully, God doesn't leave us there, lying on the side of the road with our spiritual wheels spinning. Through His Holy Spirit, He con-victs us, leads us back to the cross, and gives us the chance to return to fellowship with Him.

How we react when confronted with our sin is key. We can choose to follow the example of Adam and Eve, trying to hide from God. Or we can respond like Paul, allowing the Holy Spirit to remove our sin and fill us again.

Being convicted is not a pleasant feeling. It forces us to see parts of ourselves that we'd rather keep hidden. It brings the thoughts, attitudes, and actions we like to pretend aren't ours to the front and center.

Yet we worship a loving and gracious God. He promises us in 1 John 1:9 that if we confess our sins, he is faithful and just to forgive us our sins and to cleanse us from all unrighteousness. Ultimately, God is extending us grace when He confronts us about straying away from Him. He also provides healing and the way to be reconciled to Him.

Faith Tools

- Through a series of impossible questions, God confronts Job.
- We can overcome our hurt when we respond to conviction with repentance and thankful acceptance of God's grace.
- **Pray**: "Lord, You are the one true God. Forgive me for those times when I try to put myself in Your place." Seek to have a willing spirit that is responsive to God's conviction and grace.

Notes for Growth

Key Point I Learned Today:

_____

_____

_____

How I Want to Grow:

_____

_____

_____

My Prayer List:

_____

_____

_____

Day 58

GOD'S WAYS AREN'T OUR WAYS

"Behold, I am of small account; what shall I answer you?
I lay my hand on my mouth."
JOB 40:4 ESV

Faith Quest

Read Job 40:1–24
What is the danger of trying to make God in your own image?

Faith Trek

It's amazing how we can sometimes go to extremes in our thinking. Consider how people respond to media reports of medical research. One day we hear that eggs are high in cholesterol, so we banish them from our diets. But when we hear that high-fat/low-carb diets can help us manage our weight, eggs and bacon become our daily breakfast.

Similarly, how we think about God can lead us down some wrong paths. When we come to faith in Christ, He calls us friends (John 15:15). Our minds may take this too far, leading us to believe that, just because our human friends are like us, then God must be like us as well.

We know also that God loves us with an everlasting love. Some take that to mean that He loves in a human way, so, for example, He wants us to be happy. This is very dangerous territory, because we can then delude ourselves into believing that God approves of us breaking His commandments if it helps us achieve happiness.

In each of these cases, we have drifted away from the truth and tried to form God in our own image. We may not be bowing down to a golden calf, but the spiritual effect is ultimately the same.

The truth remains, however, that God is God and we are not. His thoughts are not the same as ours, and His ways are not our ways (see Isaiah 55:8). Forgetting this fundamental truth can lead us into sin and drive a wedge in our relationship with Him.

We are most vulnerable to thinking that God's ways are our ways when we aren't regularly hearing from Him through the Bible. Receiving the words of scripture, reflecting on their meaning, and responding to them in our lives keeps the truth of who God is and who we are in Him at the forefront. It keeps us from forgetting that we are finite but God is infinite; that we are sinful but He is holy; and that we are imperfect but He is perfect.

The fact that God's ways are not our ways should encourage us and give us reason to rejoice! Through our relationship with Him, we have access to the One who is omniscient, omnipotent, and omnipresent. It should make us want to shout with the apostle Paul, "If God is for us, who can be against us?" (Romans 8:31 ESV).

Faith Tools

- We sometimes go off track by thinking that God is the same as us.
- Remembering that God's thoughts are not our thoughts and His ways are not our ways gives a source of encouragement and hope.
- **Pray**: "Lord, let my own desire be to see You." Make a list of the scriptures that remind you that God's ways are not your ways. Keep them handy for when you find your own thinking going off track.

Notes for Growth

Key Point I Learned Today:

_____

_____

_____

How I Want to Grow:

_____

_____

_____

My Prayer List:

_____

_____

_____

FROM TURMOIL TO TRIUMPH

"Who has first given to me, that I should repay him?
Whatever is under the whole heaven is mine."

Job 41:11 esv

Faith Quest

Read Job 41:1–34
Do you believe God has the power to turn your turmoil into triumph?

Faith Trek

One of the great treasures in Nebraska is the Henry Doorly Zoo in Omaha. Occupying over 130 acres, the zoo and aquarium house more than 17,000 animals representing 962 species. You can't help but be awed by the immense variety and complexity of God's creation when you are there.

Compared to that of other animals, human's physical strength is fairly limited. For example, a tiger can climb up a ten-foot tree while hauling something weighing 1,200 pounds (twice its body weight!). African elephants are capable of carrying the equivalent of 130 grown adults. Saltwater crocodiles slam their jaws shut with a staggering force of 3,700 pounds per square inch, more than eighteen times the strength you use to tear into a good Omaha steak.

In this chapter, God used the strength of animals, a leviathan in particular, to remind Job of his weakness. God pointed out that Job had no way of subduing the leviathan. His power was limited.

This contrasts sharply with God's power. He said, "Whatever is under the whole heaven is mine."

Job had tried to reason his way out of his troubles to no avail. Yet he had no reason to despair, for the Almighty had the power to turn

Job's turmoil into triumph.

The book of Daniel contains two wonderful illustrations of God's power to deliver His servants. When Daniel was thrown into the lion's den, God closed up the mouths of the lions and Daniel survived.

In the second instance, King Nebuchadnezzar decided to punish Shadrach, Meshach, and Abednego for not worshipping him. They were condemned to be thrown into a fiery furnace. And that furnace was heated up so much that it killed the guards assigned to throw the three prisoners into it.

Nebuchadnezzar was astonished to see that the three condemned men and a fourth were walking around inside the furnace, and he called them out. This is where we find one of the most encouraging verses in scripture: "The satraps, the prefects, the governors, and the king's counselors gathered together and saw that the fire had not had any power over the bodies of those men. The hair of their heads was not singed, their cloaks were not harmed, and no smell of fire had come upon them" (Daniel 3:27 ESV).

Did you catch that? They had no smell of fire on them. Pretty amazing when you consider how pervasive the smell of smoke and fire can be.

God displayed His power in the life of Job just as He did in the lives of Daniel and his friends. And, because our God is the same yesterday, today and tomorrow, He can do the same in your life as well, turning your turmoil into triumph.

Faith Tools

- God's power is displayed through His created world and through the lives of His people.
- Whatever you are facing today, God has the power to convert your troubles into victory.
- **Pray**: "Lord, I look to You as the only One with the power to restore me." Reread Daniel 3 and spend some time reflecting on God's power at work in the lives of Daniel, Shadrach, Meshach, and Abednego.

Notes for Growth

Key Point I Learned Today:

_____

_____

_____

How I Want to Grow:

_____

_____

_____

My Prayer List:

_____

_____

_____

GOD RESTORES THE BROKENHEARTED

"I had heard of you by the hearing of the ear, but now my eye sees you."
JOB 42:5 ESV

Faith Quest

Read Job 42:1–17
How is God restoring your broken heart?

Faith Trek

We've arrived at the last chapter in Job's story. Moved by the Lord speaking to him, Job confessed that God is God and repented of his doubts and arrogance. The Lord accepted Job's confession, and their relationship was restored.

After rebuking Job's friends for their words and providing a path to reconciliation, God restored Job's fortune. Friends and family returned to him. He again became a rich man—in fact, now twice as rich as he was before. Again his wife's womb was blessed, and they welcomed seven more sons and three more daughters. Job enjoyed these blessings for another 140 years before his death.

When people talk about the book of Job, they often emphasize this last paragraph. That has always made me (Pam) a bit uncomfortable. It seems too materialistic, as if having more cattle could erase the trials Job endured. It's like saying that the joy of having these ten children would make him forget the pain of losing the others.

Certainly all of these were a blessing from God and given for Job to enjoy. But focusing on them as the source of healing misses the point. The true restoration of Job's broken heart is actually seen in verse 5. Job said that he had heard of God before, but now he had truly seen Him. He had gained a new appreciation of God's character, His holiness and

His sovereignty. His trust in God had grown. His relationship with God was deeper than ever. This is the ultimate blessing.

Faith Tools

- Through Job's repentance, his relationship with God was restored.
- God blessed Job more in his latter life than in the beginning.
- **Pray**: "Lord, I give my broken heart to You today. I'm blessed by knowing You more." Reflect on all that you have learned from your time in the book of Job. Write out how you will apply those truths to your own life.

Notes for Growth

Key Point I Learned Today:

_____

_____

_____

How I Want to Grow:

_____

_____

_____

My Prayer List:

_____

_____

_____

Notes

Day 14

    1. A portion of Arnie's testimony was adapted from Arnie Cole and Michael Ross, *Unstuck: Your Life. God's Design. Real Change* (Minneapolis: Bethany House, 2012), 24–26.

Day 15

    1. Billy Graham, *The Faithful Christian: An Anthology of Billy Graham* (New York: McCracken, 1994), 33.

Day 20

    1. Tiffany Ross, author and videographer, contributed to today's devotional entry.

Day 21

    1. Henry T. Blackaby, *Experiencing God Day-by-Day* (Nashville: Broadman & Holman, 1998), 16.

    2. C. S. Lewis, "Giving All to Christ," *Devotional Classics*, ed. Richard J. Foster and James Bryan Smith (New York: HarperCollins, 1990), 9.

Day 22

    1. Charles H. Spurgeon, *Morning and Evening* (Nashville: Thomas Nelson, 1994), December 28, evening.

    2. Freelance writer Vanessa Janusz contributed to this devotional entry.

Day 24

    1. Kenneth Barker, ed., *Reflecting God Study Bible* (Grand Rapids: Zondervan, 2000), 731.

Day 25

    1. Margie Younce, a writer and program director for a nonprofit social outreach in West Virginia, contributed this story.

Day 30

1. Richard Alleyne. "Welcome to the information age—174 newspapers a day." *The Telegraph*, February 11, 2011.

Day 32

1. Michael Ross, *Get Real, Get Ready, Get Going* (Grand Rapids: Revell, 1999), 158–59.

Day 33

1. Karen C. Hinckley, *The Story of Stories: The Bible in Narrative Form* (Colorado Springs: NavPress, 1991), 116.
2. Ibid.
3. Doug Banister, *Sacred Quest* (Grand Rapids: Zondervan, 2001), 14–15.
4. Henry Cloud, *Changes That Heal* (Grand Rapids: Zondervan, 1992), 49.

Day 35

1. C. S. Lewis Quotes, Goodreads, http://www.goodreads.com/quotes/1180-pain-insists-upon-being-attended-to-god-whispers-to-us.
2. Charles H. Spurgeon, *Morning and Evening* (Nashville: Thomas Nelson, 1994), December 28, evening.
3. Manfred Koehler, "Why Christians Suffer," *Breakaway*, March 2001, 30.

Day 36

1. Dirk Buursma and Verlyn Verbrugge, *Daylight Devotional Bible* (Grand Rapids: Zondervan, 1988), 5.

Day 41

1. Arnie Cole and Michael Ross, *Unstuck: Your Life. God's Design. Real Change* (Minneapolis: Bethany House, 2012).

Day 46

1. "Ann Landers Told Rice Myth Is for the Birds," *Houston Chronicle*, October 5, 1996, Business, 1. Read more at http://www.snopes.com/critters/crusader/birdrice.asp#euYl3HSPE2w8jIJ8.99.

Day 48

1. Tiffany Ross, author and videographer, contributed to today's devotional entry.

Day 49

1. This quote was acquired by Michael Ross through an e-mail dialogue he had with a Christian leader on June 19, 2012.

Day 50

1. Kenneth Barker, ed., *Reflecting God Study Bible* (Grand Rapids: Zondervan, 2000), 723.

2. Tess Cox contributed to today's devotional entry. She is an author, missionary, and physician's assistant in Colorado Springs.

Day 51

1. Kenneth Barker, ed., *Reflecting God Study Bible* (Grand Rapids: Zondervan, 2000), 723.

2. A. W. Tozer, *Tozer on Christian Leadership: A 366-Day Devotional* (Camp Hill, PA.: Christian Publications, 2001), reading for October 19.

3. Ibid.

Day 53

1. Karen Jensen, "The Day I Didn't Blame God," *Charisma*, August 8, 2013, http://www.charismamag.com/spirit/spiritual-growth/18315-the-day-i-didn-t-blame-god.

Day 54

1. Tiffany Ross, author and videographer, contributed to today's devotional entry.

Also available from goTandem:

Available wherever Christian books are sold.